RETURN TO ANGLIA

By the same author:

Reuben's Corner

Fall Out the Officers!

No More Soldiering for Me

Five Miles from Bunkum
(with Christopher Ketteridge)

Last Post

The Band Rats

RETURN TO ANGLIA

by

SPIKE MAYS

With drawings by Rene Eyre

LONDON
VICTOR GOLLANCZ LTD
1986

First published in Great Britain 1986
by Victor Gollancz Ltd,
14 Henrietta Street, London WC2E 8QJ

The author would like to thank Mrs Joan Lay for her kind
permission to quote from her late husband's poem on
p. 207.
'And Death shall have no Dominion' by Dylan Thomas
is published by kind permission of Messrs J. M. Dent &
Sons Ltd.

British Library Cataloguing in Publication Data
Mays, Spike
  Return to Anglia.
  1. Ashdon (Essex)—Social life and customs
  I. Title
  942.6′712   DA690.A802
  ISBN 0-575-03840-3

Photoset in Great Britain by
Rowland Phototypesetting Limited, Bury St Edmunds, Suffolk
and printed by St Edmundsbury Press
Bury St Edmunds, Suffolk

Contents

		page
1	Anticipation	7
2	Exploration	16
3	In Sickness and in Health	40
4	Praying and Preying	45
5	'Treacle' Bumpstead	52
6	Retrospection	66
7	Helions	77
8	Harking Back'ards and Forrards	83
9	Jubilation	91
10	Snobbery	96
11	Merry Molins	102
12	Hearts are Trumps!	111
13	Fruitility	119
14	The Thirst after Righteousness	123
15	Thatchin' an' Throshin'	131
16	There Was a Green Hill	136
17	Wine and Women – and One Song	144
18	Sing a Song o' Chitterlings	156
19	Time, Gentlemen, Please	160
20	My Market Guru	164
21	Probing	171
22	A Battery of Baptists	181
23	Rest on Your Arms Reversed!	186
24	Decline and . . . Fiddlesticks!	194

I

Anticipation

Suffolk born and Suffolk bred
Strong in the arm, thick in the head.

Over many years and in many lands those old words have become deeply embedded in my consciousness; linked with that longing and yearning best described by the Welsh word *hiraeth*: a bit of longing, a bit of yearning, but far deeper than either or both. In distant lands I fancied that I could see undimmed pictures of the fields, meadows, hedgerows and woodlands of my childhood. The fanciful ears of my mind could hear Suffolk birdsong, and the wonderful language of my fellow villagers: vivid reminders of the days when most villages were rather more than fair to middlin, half-tidy, or not so dusty well-brushed. Most villages were quite self-contained and self-supporting; chock-full of crafts and cunning craftsmen who supplied the wants of their people according to the standards of the time: of *my* time, in those most impressionable years. I did not want to leave East Anglia but, as they say, needs must when the devil drives.

Like most East Anglian farm-working lads at the time of the agricultural depression I sometimes went hungry. My brother had enlisted in the Grenadier Guards at the age of fifteen to bash drums and play flutes for the 1st Battalion. My friend Bill Symonds joined the Royal Horse Artillery, and both wrote home to say it was a good life with three good meals every day, lots of leisure and buglers to tell you when to get up and go to bed. Both were of the opinion that working on the land was degrading, but there was nothing else.

It was all on account of wet weather, a few heifers and a balding farmer at Place Farm in Ashdon that my career as a son of the soil was about to end. The climax came one morning when, soaked to the skin overnight, tortured with spikes of rye in my jersey, I took my body to work and the farmer quickly took me to task for being late – at half past six when it was still dark. . . .

'You're late, boy! Them heifers want their feed an' beddin'.'

'They're only beasts. I'm human!' said I in righteous indignation. 'They've food, thick coats. They're under shelter and dry. I'm soaked, since yesterday and I've had no breakfast. Bugger your heifers, I'm off home!'

Father, too ill to work after five war wounds, was not too ill to be furious.

'You oughter hev more sense, boy. You know there ain't much work about. You were lucky to hev been took on. Go straight back and apologize. Tell Bidwell you're sorry.'

Tenant farmer Bidwell, in dry clothes, under the sheltering roof of the cow byre was squatting on a stool, squirting quick jets of milk into a pail from Bella's bulger. I rested my chin on the top of the bottom half of the byre door.

'I'm back. Never meant to be rude, but I meant what I said. The heifers are dry and fed. I ain't!'

He withdrew his head from Bella's sheltering belly, turned up one of her teats and squirted milk in my eye. All smily and kind-looking.

'Thass all right, lad. Fergit it! It's hard for you. You ain't cut out fer farm wuk, God give you a bit of a brain. Find another job. Go you off home, changer clothes an' stop home in the dry. You'll hev yer wages, I know how it is.'

One week later, on Saint Patrick's Day, 17th March 1924, I said goodbye to East Anglia. At sixteen years and seven months I had been accepted as a bandboy in the regimental band of the Royal Dragoons – known today as the Blues and Royals of the Household Cavalry.

Fifty years later, on yet another Saint Patrick's Day, I retired from my press and public relations job at Heathrow Airport. I had shaken off the shackles. I felt free again, free to return to the land of the Anglo-Saxons, and I reckoned that I had the qualifications . . . I was born in Glemsford, Suffolk, on 5th August 1907 and lived there, in our bungalow near the horse-hair factory, for seven years. From 1914 to 1924 we lived in

Ashdon Place Farm

two Essex villages: Helions Bumpstead and Ashdon. Part of Ashdon, *our* part, was in Cambridgeshire. If we had tripods instead of legs, we could have plonked them down into three counties, not far from Whiten's Mere Farm. My religious qualifications were impeccable: I had been baptized at Hartest, Suffolk, immediately after my christening there. Both jobs were done for the price of one because I was puny, and the vicar thought I might not last for another service. He was not much of a prophet, for I survived long enough to be confirmed at Saint Mary's Church, Saffron Walden, Essex, and became a true East Anglian Anglican upon whose head the hands of the Bishop of Colchester had been gently laid – followed by a clout of the earhole from Mother, for tar-staining my snow-white surplice. Cleanliness is next to Godliness!

Nor was this all. I sang in church *and* chapel choirs, known as 'Devil-dodging'. They had magic lantern shows at the chapel! I attended church twice per Sabbath and Sunday school once. I never missed the Sunday school treat, which we called 'The Annual Bun Struggle', because my membership card was fully stamped for every Sunday school service. As a bit of a makeweight I sometimes got scared into going to prayer meetings and bible readings in private cottages. I learned more about Hell and Fire and Brimstone than about Heaven, and was scared stiff of God!

Then I became a soldier, after being a Bakus Boy at the Squire's Mansion, until I inadvertently chopped Butler Freeman's beehives for Estate kindling, and after farmer Bidwell discovered that I had a brain and was unsuitable for farm wuk.

I served in the army for twenty years, starting at Canterbury. I enlisted, soldiered for years in Egypt, India and Britain and loved most of it. I served throughout the Second World War and got myself war-blinded at Bayeux, that twin-towered cathedral city where Queen Mathilde stitched the Battle of Hastings. I was most interested in Bayeux: as a schoolboy in Ashdon's elementary school I was highly commended for drawing with my slate pencil a picture of Old King Harold, with an arrow stuck in his eye. Arrows were thin on the ground at Bayeux – a Jerry mortar put my eye on the blink and I feared I would never see East Anglia again. Moorfields Eye Hospital brought back my vision. Within two years I could see to study well enough to win two scholarships: to Newbattle College, Dalkeith, and the University of Edinburgh. There's boasting for you! It could never have happened had it not been for my wife Vera, who worked like a beaver to keep me in sloth and idleness, squatting on stools, just listening to pearls of wisdom from professors of Economics, English and Industrial Psychology. I met Vera in East Anglia, at my sister's wedding, thank God! In 1986 we will have been happily wed for fifty years, with six lovely grandchildren, alive, kicking and singing in Welsh Wales.

The minute I cast off the shackles of daily toil Vera developed strange ideas about settling down. To lend force to her wish she croaked a few bars of her national anthem . . . *'Hen wlad fy Nhadau'* – 'Land of my fathers'.

'Hellabit,' said I. 'We'll settle down in the land of *my* father: in Silly Suffolk where I was born. We only have one father apiece. Put on your house-hunting boots, we're moving!'

We had no intention of leaving right away. We had lived in Middlesex for many years, to be near my work at Heathrow

Airport, where we had many friends. I was Secretary of the Hayes and Harlington Arts Council and, more important, I was honoured by becoming President of the Thames Valley Suffolk Society.

Except for our Suffolk origin we were a mixtie-maxtie in terms of occupation. Chairman Ernie Pierce owned a news-paper and tobacconist's and was a Justice of the Peace. We boasted a brace of welfare officers, a clutch of teachers, a covey of nurses, voluntary hospital workers and a male midwife. Ex-policemen and ex-servicemen abounded. Only one ex-horse ploughman: a great man for growing vegetables from his own compost. Everything 'left over' was consigned to his compost-heap, even the dustbin presented by the council. We managed to recruit a few secretaries, two telephonists, a bevy of capable housewives and a professional bird-watcher. Dotted about in pleasant and less pleasant places in the Thames Valley, most dwelt in Teddington, Sipson, West Drayton, Hounslow, Twickenham, Hayes, Harlington, Harrow, Woolwich, Rich-mond, Cranford, Isleworth, Lee and Kenton. All were born in East Anglia, mostly in Suffolk . . . Ipswich, Glemsford, Monks Eleigh, Hadleigh, Lavenham, Long Melford, Cavend-ish, Clare, Sudbury, Woodbridge, Bury St Edmunds – with a brace of 'foreigners' from East Bergholt and an ex-reed thatcher from Swaffham.

At each of our meetings we tried something different. Hush prevailed when recordings were played of the Suffolk dialect. Most of them were made by a good Welshman who lives near Norwich but is renowned as the best Suffolk folklorist: my good friend George Ewart Evans who wrote *The Pattern under the Plough*, *Ask the Fellows who Cut the Hay*, *The Horse in the Furrow* and others. George still writes to me, in Welsh!

Eyes seldom blinked as we sat silent for ciné films of Con-stable country and heard the birdsong. We got to know each other very well – particularly a stranger who came one night from his statistician's office in Heathrow Airport. Bill was an amateur bird-watcher of international renown and was far more interested in the plumage of the common starling than in the livery of the sixty-eight airline companies.

Late one summer, we gathered for the traditional Horkey Feast: the old harvesters' own supper to celebrate the end of harvest. In our Hounslow hall we could hear the overhead thundering and whine of jet aircraft. Not quite the right music, but the sight of the tables brought us back to sense. Our 'mawthers' had cooked all the 'vittels' and tarted up the tables with corn dollies, home-made cottage loaves shaped like cornsheaves surrounded with corn posies: heads of wheat, barley, oats and rye. On the snow-white linen, boats and vases of wild flowers separated dwarfish farm labourers fashioned from vegetables in season – all sartorially splendid in hand-stitched cotton smocks and straw hats.

On side tables, as had been the custom in village pubs and on village greens, were stacked the good things from Mother Earth, with nary a tin or tin-opener in sight. Ponderous pump-kins squatted alongside majestic marrows and scrubbed spuds: 'King Teddies' all pinky of eye and 'Kidneys', all purply and polish. Cabbages and cauliflowers, as round and solid as Cromwellian cannon-balls; carnations and carrots, radishes and roses, parsnips and pears, apples and artichokes and strings of mighty onions. For the 'sweet of tooth' there were castles of preserves turreted with jars of clover honey, jam, crab-apple and quince jellies. For the meat-eaters there was crispy-rinded pork, and cold beef; to be 'helped down' from a turret of pickles – onion, beetroot, cabbage and 'to bring 'em out in a muck sweat' some sauce-boats of horse-radish. 'Washed down' with brimming tankards of Greene King ale, we always ended with a prayer and the usual brace of seasonal hymns . . . 'We plough the fields and scatter . . .' and 'Come, ye thankful people, come, raise the song of Harvest Home'. And I each time remembered our choirboy version . . .

> All is safely gathered in,
> If it ain't, it oughter bin.
> All upon the barnyard floor,
> For the rats an' meece to gnaw.

My mind was taken back to my very first Horkey Feast. It was held at the Bonnett Inn, Ashdon. I felt so proud because I had been given the seat of honour – next to old Toe-rag. He was the horse-keeper and our Lord of the Harvest and I was horse-leader for the wagons on Woodshot field. Toe-rag had told me I was a good 'shrieker and hollerer' and asked me to say grace at the end of the supper. But I could not. I was so emotionally disturbed by the lovely singing that I completely forgot the simple words: 'We thank the Lord for what we've had.' I shall never forget them again!

Our Thames Valley Suffolk Society was not rich, except in memories. Our funds were garnered by raffling gifts from members ranging from bundles of yard-long leeks and parsnips and pickling cabbages to tape-recordings, East Anglian magazines and books by East Anglian writers. We were permanently solvent, even after raising enough financial wind to waft us back to Suffolk at least once a year.

One year we decided to beat the bounds by coach and visit the glorious River Stour. After a good lunch in Colchester we moved off to Nayland to visit the birthplace of our first-rate secretary Mrs Winfield. We went to her church and were heartened to see the pleasure on her face as she knelt in her old pew to say a homecoming prayer. Then off through the land of the high horizon for our circular tour: East Bergholt, Copdock, Hintlesham, Hadleigh, Kersey, Chelsworth, Monks Eleigh, Lavenham, Long Melford, and Sudbury. Not a wisp of cloud was in the sky. Potatoes were in white and purple flower. Light wind rustled the yellowing barley, and our lovely land looked, smelt, felt its Sunday best.

Along the River Stour we followed a course which has been traversed by barge, train, many fine horses, and now, the smelly death-dealing motor-car. Not far from the towpath along which horses had plodded to tug barges before the 'iron horse' had ousted them, the signs of the times became regrettably evident. John Constable's East Bergholt had become commercialized: where the boundary river meanders quietly between gentle green banks, softly screened by the draping tendrils of weeping willow, on the way to Flatford Mill; at the beginning of the high-hedged and tree-banked lane leading to Flatford Mill and Willy Lot's cottage.

'Howd you hard! You carn't goo no fu'ther. It's Shanks's Pony from here on!' said a misery in Chief Constable blue.

A second coachload of ancient Suffolkers was halted. We proceeded on foot, supporting an eighty-year-old lady who complained about motor-cycles whizzing past with 'bits of hussies, half-naked an' transistors blarin'", as pillion passengers.

Constable Blue let us into the secret. . . .

'Carn't do nuthin' about it. Flatford Mill is now in the hands of the protective National Trust, whatever that might be. Bloody hot, ain't it!'

On the bridge wall sat a man with horny hands, wide eyes and that look of a man who knows about horses.

'Good afternoon,' said I. 'You look like a man who can draw a furrow.'

'That I can. For nigh on fifty year. Started as a boy. Wooden plough, a pair o' Suffolks, cord rein. Don't need cords fer Suffolks. You jest talk to 'em. "Gee, now!" That means goo to the right; and "Walkamellor" to goo to the left. Draw every furrow jest on their own; straight as a die. Not a mite o' vice in 'em. Metty. Hard wuk, seventy-hour week, all weathers, fer lessen two quid. That's if you're the hoss-keeper. Others got less, even shepherds an' cattle men.'

I told him that I knew because I had worked on the land as a boy for ten bob a week. That I was thinking of returning to Suffolk . . . 'I think it's a glorious county, don't you?'

'Not now. Hellabit! It was, and we were happier. It's only glorious f'that lot lookin' arter motors in that medder. A good five hund'ed on 'em parked there a-drippin' oil over the grass. Might be glorious fer the medder owner, they pay he eighty pee an hour!'

'You don't approve!'

'That I don't. Hate it! Motors, tractors, aeroplanes an' combine-harvesters. All that row. Can't hear the birds a-singin'. Things ain't right when you can't hear the birds!'

Terry Hext, a master builder, offered to buy our house in Hayes. He liked it, and so he should. He was a school-friend of my son John, and when his wife slung him out he arrived at our house, very late at night, and asked if we could put him up for the weekend. We put him up, and we should be in *The Guinness Book of Records*. He stayed with us for a very long weekend – fifteen years.

Vera and I house-hunted in the Land of my Father, aided and abetted by my brother Les, who lived in Haverhill, Suffolk, brother Jack, who lived at Stetchworth, nearer to Newmarket, Suffolk, and brother Frank who had his habitat at Saffron Walden, Essex. Then one day we had fine news from sister-in-law Bessie – Brother Leslie's wife and schoolgirl sweetheart.

'There is a lovely bungalow at Steeple Bumpstead,' wrote Bessie, and sent us a photograph. We came, we saw, and we were conquered.

2

Exploration

From a fellow-Suffolker with whom I had much in common I had expected to get a morsel of enthusiasm about my return. We had served in the army for many years, in many lands and were PRO persons at the same airport at the same time.

Maybe he was displeased that Duggy Saunders of Uxbridge who had not been a soldier or PRO had kindly driven me to many Suffolk places during the previous nine months, to help in my search for a home. Although born in Middlesex and living near us, he was Suffolk-crazy. His only other love in life was the circus, and tearing circus posters from Suffolk bill-boards. He was a retired insurance broker and it was said that under his bed were boxes packed with swiped circus bills and notices, all heavily insured. Duggy was almost as inquisitive as he was security-conscious. But his was a kindly curiosity, because he thought I could help him in his prowls for Suffolk folklore. He carried more keys than a prison warder, was a double locker-upper who locked himself in and out of diverse places daily.

I told Duggy about the fields that my grandfather and I had worked on in Ashdon, Essex; that every field had its own name: Old Lay, New Lay, Sparks's, Thruskels, Long Mead, Short Mead, Holden, Woodshot, Little Bourne, Great Bourne, Hungerton, Bartlow and many more. Duggy was not impressed; possibly because the names were not on Suffolk bill-boards advertising a circus. I told him that I also loved Essex, that there were good places in Essex where they had fairs and galas every year and sometimes a circus. Not only that, their names had been used to make a place-name poem . . .

> Willingale Doe and Willingale Spain,
> Bulvan and Bobbingworth, Colne Engaine;
> Wenden Lofts, Beaumont-cum-Mose, Bung Row,

Gestingthorpe, Ugley and Fingringhoe;
Helions Bumpstead and Mountnessing,
Bottle End, Tolleshunt D'Arcy, Messing;
Islands of Canvey, Foulness, Potton,
Stondon Massey and Belchamp Otton;
Ingrave and Ingworth and Inworth and Kedington,
Shallow Bowels, Ulting and Kelvedon;
Margaret Boothing and Manningtree –
The bolder you sound 'em, the better they be.

Duggy was slightly interested, only because these villages
held a circus now and again. I promised to send him a four-
hundred-year-old description of the county, but he did not live
to see it, alas!

This shire is moste fatt, and full of profitable thinges,
exceeding (as far as I can finde) anie other SHIRE, for the
generall commodeties and the plentie.
Though Suffolk be more highlie commended of some wher-
with I am not yet aquaynted. But this Shire seemeth to me
to deserve the tital of the English Goshen, the fattest of the
Lande, comparable to Palestine.
But I cannot commende the healthfulness of it.
And especiallie nere the sea coast, Rochford, Denge, Tenter-
ing Hundredes, and other low places abut the creekes, which
gave me a moste cruel quarterne fever. But the manie and
sweete commodeties counter-vale the danger.

(Norden, 1594)

'I'll drive you to Norwich, Spike. We can spend a day or
two in Suffolk on the way up, and down!'
I had been invited to appear on an Anglia TV programme
Bygones. All I knew about Norwich was that, undeservedly, it
is the capital of East Anglia when to my mind, it should have
been 'Glorious Glemsford'. Norfolk reeds also came to mind,
and the havoc they caused to puny hands in the cold, wet and
perishing process of 'yelving', a hand-combing of reeds and
straw prior to thatching.
En route, we took in Ashdon. Its natural beauty has not
changed. As in my boyhood, artists with oils, water-colours,
pencils and crayons arrive in springtime and autumn trying to

capture snippets of the masterpiece, but there are changes. Once sparse, the population has increased, but with fewer children. Eight to twelve children was the family norm during my childhood. New houses have been built by local builders who have enhanced the beauty in some places but, for me, not in others. Where once was wilderness throbbing with life in tangles of overgrown hedgerows, profusions of wild flowers and wonderful birdsong from finch, tit, warbler, linnet and lark, the croak of the moorhen and rainbow flashes from kingfishers, there are 'improvements'. Tidiness prevails, neatness abounds and the village has won awards for The Best Kept Village.

Communication has improved since the two village pumps have been uprooted. No more do the women scuttle off all shoulder-yoked and galvanized-bucketed for water and gossip. Crystal clear spring water is now 'on tap' in every cottage and if Mrs 'A' is bursting to tell Mrs 'B' what Mrs 'Y' said about Mrs 'Z' at the Women's Institute, she has only to dial Mrs 'B's' number. Most mawthers are now on the phone. In the 'Ends' of the village, there are Swiss chalets with all mod. cons, including multi-coloured crazy-paving 'twixt little plots of short-cropped lawnlets; like portions pinched from the Centre Court of Wimbledon or Sheffield snooker tables. Our lovely dialect is fading through the infiltration of townsmen – those who wish to settle down in their declining years. Mechanization has eliminated the drudgery from labour on the land and our dark heavy soil continues to produce magnificent wheat, cereals of lesser royalty and excellent root crops for cattle bait and sugar-making.

Fortunately, the old order remains and the local villagers set the standard. For me this remains the most important feature, the real meaning of village life. It is the country community that provides almost everyone else with not only the basic facilities and amenities of life, but that all-important corporate sense that arises from proximity and daily association. In other words . . . 'We all know one another and we get on tidy well.'

I am glad I wor brung up in Ashdon!

I wanted to show Duggy Bragg's Mill: only a couple of meadow widths from our brick and flint tied cottage which my father had christened 'Brick and Stone Villa'.

Walt's cottage and Granny's cottage next to 'Brick and Stone Villa'

This fine post mill stands as a landmark on the highest point of Ashdon village. It remains more than a landmark for me. My lifelong friend Christopher Ketteridge and I called it our Windmill University. Night after night and long into the night we had read there and studied, getting to grips with Autosuggestion, the brainchild of M. Coué, and convinced ourselves according to his creed that . . . on every day and in every way we were gradually getting better and better. Nor was this all. Christopher had purchased twelve long grey books. For months afterwards we were dedicated to the study of Pelmanism, a time-devouring but absorbing undertaking from which we both profited.

Duggy was delighted to learn about this, but more so when I recounted how, from the top sail of that old mill, Christopher and I brought the new 'wireless' to Ashdon village . . . all the way from 2LO at Savoy Hill.

After erecting a long phosphor-bronze aerial from the top-most mill-sweep we wrote to Selfridges for a kit of parts and one pair of head-phones. We then made the first cat's-whisker set in the village. We twiddled its whisker for weeks, to receive nothing but hush. We sent back the crystal. It was a dud. When we twiddled with the new one, to our surprise and delight we heard faint strains of music and a human voice proclaiming . . . 'This is Henry Hall!' We searched adjacent fields, hoping to find someone to share our joy. We found Walt Nunn, whose pet expressions were . . . 'There's no mistake', and 'A bit of a caution'. Walt was a horse-keeper, who looked like one of his horses.

We clapped our precious head-phones over his hairy ears and watched his bushy brows rise in wonderment.

'Coo!' said Walt . . . 'Thasser bit of a caution, there's no bloody mistake! From London, yew say? I don't bloody well believe it!'

'Stop swearing, Walt,' said Christopher. 'Do you know that with those phones on, every word you say can be heard in London!'

Walt tore off the phones. 'Bugger that fer a tale. But if they owd cockneys start tellin' tales about me an' my Missus, I'll hev the bloody coppers arter 'em mighty sharp!'

Duggy was delighted. We moved to Brick and Stone Villa. The name had been altered to Flint Cottage. I pointed to my old bedroom window. Duggy took pictures, then asked . . . 'Is that bend near the Bonnett your Reuben's Corner, then?'

'No, Duggy. The corner is inside the pub. For sixty years my paternal grandfather Reuben Ford was horse-keeper at Overhall Farm, just at the top of Overhall Lane. Each day he had his midday pint there, to wash down his bread and cheese and slice of raw onion. He had his own pint pot, his own stool and he always sat in the fireplace corner. He was very proud of that spot, he called it his own. It was important to him for he owned little. Even if the pub was filled and his stool the only seat unoccupied no one else would sit there. If someone tried he'd be told mighty sharp . . . "You marn't sit there, metty. That's Reuben's Corner!"'

'So you named your book after a farm labourer's drinking stool in a village pub! I thought it was the corner of the road leading to Castle Camps,' said Duggy with wondering eyes.

'You're not the only one, Duggy boy. Charabanc-loads and

coach-loads of people have, from all over the British Isles, been lost for weeks, just looking for that famous corner where a wonderful man supped his pint. You have been rude to my dear old grandad. Get behind that wheel. We will now go to Haverhill and I will introduce you to my brother Leslie. Don't upset *him* – he is very sensitive and was once in the boxing team of the Grenadier Guards.'

Brother Leslie, ex-thick-ear-specialist, was out. So we drove on to Great Wratting, Suffolk, to see my friend Christopher Ketteridge, who was busy writing a poem to put in our book *Five Miles from Bunkum* which described in detail the arts and crafts, and the highly skilled craftsmen we had known in the village of Ashdon. On the way I told Duggy how very much Christopher had helped me when I was a lad, and that was one of the reasons I wished to return to Anglia. After Agnes (Christopher's wife) had plied us with her culinary delights and first-class home-made wines, Duggy said he too would like to return to Anglia, every day.

We stayed that night at Great Wratting's pub-cum-post-office, The Red Lion, where landlord-cum-postmaster Stan Coe invited me to preach the sermon for the Horkey Supper. Welsh persons were present, including one ex-Commander Morgan of the Royal Navy who had helped to pull the plug out of the German battleship *Scharnhorst*. We dined and wined, sang like linnets before going to bed, then Duggy discovered he had locked his car keys in his pyjama suitcase which he had locked before inadvertently locking his car. He slept in the raw for a change, but we were up in time for the dawn chorus, which the birds continued for us throughout a marvellous breakfast. We were in Suffolk. Duggy was delighted!

We drove on through the wool towns and villages, Stoke-by-Clare, Clare, Cavendish and Long Melford, all alongside the beautiful boundary separating Essex from Suffolk, the River Stour. I told Duggy of the war that once raged between my birthplace, Glemsford (Little Egypt) and Long Melford. Glemsford was a hive of Liberal inclination and action, Melford a Tory stronghold. On Saturday evenings the 'Egyptians' would 'cut across the fields' to Melford to have a political punch-up with the Tories. On the next Saturday the Tories would stroll off to Glemsford to return the compliment. Sometimes the gutters ran with blood, but the police were unable to cope with the weekly uprisings.

The words Glemsford and Egypt were so synonymous that 'Religion' became involved. One day in a Long Melford Sunday school a religious instructor was taken aback.

'Now, Belinda dear. Tell the class where they took the Little Lord Jesus when King Herod started to kill all the firstborn.'

'Please Miss, they took him to *Glemsford*!'

Since then remarkable changes have altered both places very considerably. Commercialism has reared its head. Practically all the shops in that long, long street which put the 'long' into Long Melford have descended to the selling of souvenirs; the most enterprising displaying an up-to-date notice . . .

ANTIQUES – MADE WHILE YOU WAIT!

I wanted to go to Sudbury, but after Duggy had unlocked the face of his watch, we had not the time. I was hoping to visit ninety-four-year-old Ernest Ambrose who wrote a marvellous book, *Melford Memories* – one I felt honoured to review for him. At each of his several invitations I had other engagements. He died on that day I was Norwich-bound with Duggy.

Anglia Television and friendly co-founder Dick Joice could not have given a more positive welcome. After the wining and dining Dick presented me with mammoth photographs, some taken in Glemsford when I was three clad in petticoat, with scarlet sash, white furry hat as I clutched a scruffy teddy bear; others were of my family, friends, workmates, with one Anglican vicar and a Baptist parson.

After being quizzed, questioned, interrogated and partly inquisitioned by Dick we watched the show go out, in Anglia's studio. We slept and breakfasted at the Castle Hotel, Norwich.

Duggy seemed somewhat unsettled at breakfast. Between bites of marmaladed buttered toast and quick gulps of very hot coffee, he was scanning a roadmap propped before him on sauce bottles.

'It's gone nine and we ought to get moving. I'd like to be in Clare for lunch. Which is the quickest way?'

'Get on the motorway, the A11. Aim the bonnet at Wymondham, then Thetford, where you change to the A143 and aim at Bury St Edmunds, the capital of West Suffolk. Nip smartly

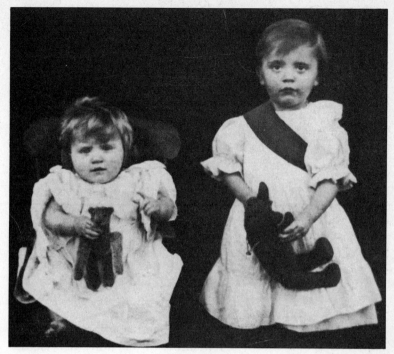

Spike (wearing sash) and brother Leslie

through Bury to the A134 and we'll be in Long Melford in time to water our nags by opening time, and in Clare before closing time. How's that?'

'That will be just right,' said Duggy. But it did not turn out just right. We drove on the right roads, with Duggy grousing about the uninteresting flatness of Norfolk and how glad he would be to get to Clare. We reached Long Melford and turned due east for Clare, and then the fun started . . . as we neared Cavendish he braked, stopped and hollered . . . 'Look, Spike!'

'Look where?'

'That notice, GLEMSFORD . . . where you were born. Up that road to the right. Let's go and have a look.'

I was not keen. My mind still bore the scars of some of that privation we had endured during the agricultural depression, and the start of the Great War.

'Please!' hollered Duggy.

We motored up the hill, my mind filled with voices long

since silenced. I thought of my mother's courage and fortitude; how she had gleaned beans at sixpence a bushel and picked stones from the fields for less to keep us alive; how she had christened our little bungalow Kuldysack, because it stood at the end of Mill Lane.

Memories cascaded back. I fancied I could still smell the hair. I sniffed, I *could* smell horse-hair – just like the smell when I was only three. I used to sit with my head through the railings, trying to get to the heart and soul of smells. Strong soap was one. Wet hair was another. There were strange noises, clouds of white, wet steam and lots of men far too busy to tell me what was going on in the steamy, noisy, smelly world.

My father and mother used to sleep on a mattress made from horse-hair. I found out by exploration. A little leather pad had come off the mattress and left a hole. I could see bits of hair and spent a lovely afternoon pulling them out. Some were grey, some dark and light brown, but the best were reddish gold from the coats of chestnut horses. Father told me . . . 'The men are cleaning the dirty hair of dead horses to make mattresses, cushions and pillows.' Then he slapped my backside. Perhaps that is why I remember the old horse-hair factory so well. . . .

We halted, smack outside the bungalow. It was trim with fresh paint and the garden filled with flowers. I could 'feel' the inside!

Duggy pulled out his map and started surveying. Then the head of a lady I took to be middle-aged came to the window. She wore a scarf over her silvered hair. She spoke. Her voice was angelic . . . pure Suffolk, as she pointed to Duggy's maps.

'Yew ain't lorst, are yew? Yew carn't goo no fu'ther, it's a blind alley. Yew carn't tun rownd, thass tew narrer. Yew'll hev t' back owt, boy; but dew yew watch owt fer they grut stuns!'

'Thank you!' said I. 'We are not lost, just having a look round. See that bungalow? I was born in it sixty years ago.'

'Sixty year, yew say?'

'Yes, just over that, and I've never been back to look at it till now.'

'Well, I never did! See that one at the end, t'other side?

Well I wor born in it over sixty-foive year agoo, and I ain't never left it.'

She had smooth skin, a ruddy complexion and silvery silken hair. Until she screwed up her face to squint me a closer inspection, not a wrinkle.

'Are yew one o' they Mays's, then? If you are I knew yar father. He were the village postman afore he went orf to Canada!'

'I am his eldest son. He's dead now, but I am delighted to meet you. Hop in the car and we'll go for a drink and a chat.'

'I carn't fare t'dew that. Gotta git back ter wuk!'

'Surely you are not working at sixty-five, m'dear!'

'Sartinly, look at me hands.'

From finger-tips to wrists her hands were bright dry scarlet. Perhaps she's been wine-making, I thought, for the red was too bright for beetroot.

'What's that stain?'

''Tain't stain, boy. Tha's dye. We wor a-bleachin' on 'em yisterday, and dyein' on 'em terday.'

'Bleaching and dyeing what?'

'Hoss-hair.'

'For what?'

'Sojers' hats. Plumes an' such fer they owd helmets.'

'Do you send them to the Household Cavalry?'

'Sartinly!'

'To my old regiment, the Blues and Royals?'

'Dunno bowt that, but they do say the hoss sojers don't pay. They send us the hair, y'see, an' we supply the bleach an' dye; so that's even stevens, like. But they do pay in other ways. . . . They send us all the hoss-shit. Good job, too, or we shoun't git a lotter mushrooms. Like us owd 'uns, there ain't many on us abowt, nor hoss-shit neither!'

We backed out, keeping a sharp lookout for 'they grut stuns' (great stones).

'Fancy that,' said Duggy. 'She knew your father and she sends helmet plumes to our old regiment. We won't stop at Clare. Let's go back to Ashdon. Something is bound to happen, or someone turn up, after that lot!'

'Her lovely language!' said I, more to myself than to Duggy. 'Do you realize that I didn't even ask her name. She speaks like the old Suffolkers I knew as a boy. They didn't speak, they sang. Every sentence seemed like bits of anthems we used to sing in the choir.'

'Do you mean Christopher and his poetry? Has he written much of it?'

'No, Duggy, no! I was talking about the lovely hoss-shit lady and her voice. Christopher introduced me to his Latin poetry when I was a schoolboy.' Now this was true, but I didn't tell Duggy the details. It was through Christopher that my real education began, in the back-yard of an Ashdon pub, now called a Cromwellian Coach House, which it had been, but is now The Rose and Crown. At school dinner break I used to go to the former coach house which had been converted into a builder's workshop, where Christopher Ketteridge – six years my senior – and apprenticed to his father York as a bricklayer – would be mixing cement. Christopher was a fine scholar who had won scholarships but could not afford to take

Christopher Ketteridge, my childhood friend

them up. He used to draw murals with lumps of charcoal and write poetry on the white plaster panels between the oak-timbered stud work. No sooner did father York's eyes light upon them than they would disappear under a couple of deft swipes of his three-pronged distemper brush. One poem earned York's respect and stayed. It appeared to be written in Latin. Christopher and I used to recite it each time we met but I did not understand a word for weeks;

> *Sedito sali cum sedi anita longa mi.*
> *Fors uper abit o meta pio vel summamante.*
> *Foro midea miartis ures O cantu care forme?*
> *No tature nota bene jo no dux nopes ome.*
> *O cari cantat allino tos super longae.*
> *O misere mi salis dum no donna mor tome.*
> *O mari aggi molle cum anita mihite.*

One day Christopher told me how he had found it printed in a time-yellowed copy of *John o' London's Weekly*, given to him in a bundle of papers by the matron of the Waifs' and Strays' Home (now more politely known as The Orphanage). We have laughed about the simple interpretation for as long as we have been firm friends – sixty-eight years.

> Said I to Sally, come, said I, and eat along of me.
> For supper a bit of meat, a pie of veal, some ham and tea.
> For O, my dear, my heart is yours. O, can't you care for
>   me?
> No tater, not a bean, Joe. No ducks, no peas, O me!
> O care I can't at all, I know, to sup along of he.
> O misery, my Sally's dumb, no donna more to me.
> O Mary, Aggie, Molly, come and eat of my high tea.

As we motored quietly along the Stour, I recalled how my Windmill Professor had taught me to remember never to forget; his teaching of the perils of intelligence was unorthodox. High on the list were observation, concatenation and recollection, and it worked. I began to take real interest in, and notice of, folk, creatures, birds, flowers, crops, fields and footpaths: even to counting the nails in farmhands' clodhoppers and in

their garden gates and fences. I could find my way in dense
fog and notice the difference in ordinary sounds when the fog
obscured and altered noise and places. Each night I would be
tested, before we took out our books to the candle-lit mill
loft. We read Edgar Wallace mysteries; Rider Haggard's fine
adventure stories, and chunks from *Macbeth* with owls hooting
around us and Nipper Marsh's dogs yelping down below in
the village to get the 'effect' right. In a few months I will be
back again, to the place where real life began for me, I thought,
and relished that thought.

We told our friends in the Thames Valley Suffolk Society
of our impending translation. All were pleased for us, some
envious. Ted Roscher had to be different. He was my very
good friend, the PRO of Air France, a true Suffolker. One
who put on a posh accent when conversing with the upper
crust. With me he was natural and reverted to his native
tongue. When peeved his moustache bristled: a long and
mighty affair he had nurtured whilst serving twelve years in
the Suffolk Regiment (The Dirty Dozen), 12th of Foot. To
the lovely air hostesses of Air France, at home and abroad, he
was Major Moustachio.

'Going to Steeple Bumpstead to end your days, my owd
met! You must be as daft as lights. It's right off the map and
there's bugger-all there. One church, one chapel and only two
pubs when there used to be five. They've got two shops and
half of one of 'em is a post-office. Once you're in the village
you'll never get out again. No railway, mate. A bus to Saffron
Walden once daily, but you hev to walk back. The Premier
travel coach goes to Haverhill twice a week for shoppers; full
of old buggers like you, natterin' women with prams an'
shoppin' baskets on wheels. All women an' wheels! The people
you used to know in the villages hev been kickin' up daisies
fer years. You'll hev no friends, metty, as sure as God made
little apples. I wouldn't goo there for all the bloody tea in
China.'

'Thanks a lot! Aren't you going to wish us good luck?'

Ted winked, put out his hand and said, 'The best of British
mate; and by Christ you're going to need it!'

Long before Major Moustachio had tried to put a damper
on my return, and for many times, friend Duggy had whisked

Our Windmill University, Ashdon

me back for house-hunting. He tried to disguise the fact that
he was more anxious than me to leave Middlesex . . . 'We
could look round Suffolk, spend a day or two here and there.
Have a look at your old haunts and you compare the differences. I'd like to see where you worked and the people you
worked with.'

Two days later we were in the south-western corner of Suffolk.
After an excellent lunch at The Bell Hotel, Clare, we motored
slowly and inquisitively towards Ashdon, Essex, where I hoped
to find 'owd mets' who had not kicked up a daisy.

'We'll soon be in Cavendish,' said Duggy as he polished the
windscreen with his brand new Suffolk wash-leather. 'Oh no,
you won't metty,' said I. 'You're driving away from it. Turn
right about, aim your motor at Long Melford and you'll see
lovely Cavendish on your nearside.'

Some magnetic influence seemed to be working on me;
drawing me back to where I had been born; giving me butter-
flies in the belly and a feeling of comforting elation. We were
on that road to Cavendish, one which seemed to saunter or
glide along the soothing waters of the Stour. Presently, we
were admiring that delightful L-formation of thatched and
plastered cottages on that famous green which now rivals
Kersey as the most attractive and much photographed rustic
scene in Suffolk. Each cottage seemed to have its own individual glow, like a pinkied sunset; all topped up like a beautiful
woman with a crowning glory of magnificent thatch.

In 1956 they were in deteriorating disrepair, but were restored and saved by the craftsmanship and collected pennies
of the stalwart folk of kindly Cavendish. So well indeed that
in 1960 Cavendish collected a trophy for 'the best kept village
in Suffolk', and like an overnight mushroom a sign of commem-
oration was erected by villagers to lighten the unenlightened.

'Why are so many Suffolk houses painted pink?' asked
Duggy.

'It's all on account of the sloes,' said I.

'Sloes?' queried Duggy, looking mighty mystified . . .
'Sloes!'

'Yes siree, sloes, the fruit of the blackthorn; the only thing
to use for making sloe gin, and if you ain't tasted sloe gin made
by a good Suffolk mawther, you ain't lived!'

'It's *very* good. I've had some – but what's it got to do with pink paint?'

'Everything! . . . Long before our great grandfathers were pupped most of our village cottages were "of clay and wattles made . . .". The clay, or plaster was not quite the finishing. The outsides were then "daubed", the process of plastering. Not the plastering you achieve after downing a jar or two of sloe gin. Some say that Constable Pink was created by mixing the clay and daub with the juice of the sloe. It was the colour of the mortar sloshed on by craftsmen plasterers with wooden trowels before they tarted up the walls by pargeting. The juice of the sloe was the colouring agent or dye.'

'Pargeting! What's that?'

'I'll show you some of the best when we get to Saffron Walden.'

'I like that very much.'

'What, pargeting?'

'No! I mean the juice of the slow . . . "The Juice of the Sloe" would make a lovely name for a village pub.'

'If we don't get moving we shall not reach Ashdon before closing time and there'll be "no juice for the slow"! Get cracking!'

'What road are we on?'

'The Cambridge–Colchester, A604. Toss up for the route. Heads to Haverhill, tails to Castle Camps and Bartlow. If we are too late for Ashdon, we can snatch a snifter in Bartlow's famous pub, The Three Hills.'

Owned by Greene King, the brewers of Bury St Edmunds, Bartlow's Three Hills stands on the borders of Essex and Cambridgeshire and gained its title from three ancient mounds. Originally there were five of these peculiar bumps, but one or more were removed in 1865 for the proposed track of the Great Shelford–Marks Tey railway. The tradition persists that they date from the battle between Edmund Ironside and Canute, but excavations in the mid-nineteenth century disclosed first-century Roman walled graves containing glass ornaments and highly decorated bronzes and enamels. They are reputedly the largest burial mounds in Europe, the greatest being forty feet high and a hundred and forty-five feet long.

I well remember when Christopher Ketteridge and I undertook prohibited exploration. We were scared stiff and sensed a strange, almost eerie quietening influence. We were reminded of the village tales of bygone ages and men long since dead, as indeed is apt, for they are the graves of Roman warriors. Castle Camps and Shudy Camps, the next villages on the way to Bartlow's Three Hills, were supposed to have been the camping places of many a Roman Legion. Now and again old horse-ploughmen would unearth some relic or coin, to prove something or other, if only a new topic of conversation in the village pub.

I was not unduly interested in Romans. I wanted to have a peep at Shudy Camps. We could see the old church standing on the junction of Bartlow Road and Broad Street, the narrowest lane in Shudy. Those fertile fields over which I had so often plodded in my heavily-hobnailed clod-hoppers seemed to have expanded, but something most important was missing. The trees! . . . Not only the trees but those wonderful high hedges and flower-bedecked verges. Shocked and quite hurt, I began to sing that song, the anthem to desecration, 'Where have all the flowers gone?'

'Are you all right, Spike?' asked Duggy.

'No! Drive to that road junction and I'll tell you why.'

I tried to explain. Even though Duggy and I had toured East Anglia quite extensively, I had failed dismally to notice or appreciate the degree of spoliation and inconsideration to which our lovely countryside had been subjected. Here, in Shudy Camps, I was on the borders of my own midden, that vital part of my childhood and boyhood which I had known and loved so well. I knew the names of every field and meadowland, of every footpath, glade and lane. Along those old roads were high hedges, twelve to twenty feet. Daffodils, primroses, wild hyacinths, dog-daisies and violets used to cover banks and verges, creating carpets of colour to brighten our springtime and summery days. In golden cornfields poppies waved their scarlet banners. With briars as thick as a boy's arm clusters of dog-roses put out the pink and white petals, as though caressing the scarlet and orange of the previous year's hips and haws: all inextricably intertwined with Old Man's Beard, convolvulus and bellbine. I remembered how, as boys, we used to pick and cherish bellbines and 'cixies', for we used to cut them into cigarette and cigar lengths and smoke the stuff. We endured blistered tongues and the pain of scorched tonsils, for it was 'manly' to smoke. Cigarettes were beyond our financial reach. Five Woodbines cost tuppence.

My father had taught me hedging and ditching, to keep bill-hooks and sickles razor-sharp and make the cleanest of cuts on each severed twig. First, we would pull out dead wood, then cut back and bend back new growth, keeping the tops and sides even to help the hedge to thicken the following year. Hedgerows were eye-openers, adventure places, full of interest as well as the many small creatures sheltering and feeding in them. They were made up of a variety of plants with their own characters and habits. Yellow tassellings of the hazel, the male flowers and, on the same shrub, those tiny flower-tips of the female – waiting for the hedgers, birds, bees or beasts, to shake down the pollen from the drooping yellowness, to fertilize them and bring forth delicious hazel-nuts. They included the angular twigs of the elder, with nice straight growths of new wood between the nodal joints, just waiting for us boys to make pop-guns from them. There were dogwood, privet, hawthorn, sloe and crab-apple: the first for making long-lasting walking sticks; the sloe and crab-apple for wine or delicious jelly. Also to delight the eye were wild peas, or tufted vetch, all kinds of ivy – some flowering in autumn and winter and fruiting in spring – plus that soft red moss growing on the briars of wild roses – Old Robin's Pin-cushion. Through each month of the year there were the hedgerows' fruit and flowers, waiting to be discovered by novices and townsmen; always there to be seen, loved and understood by the countryman. There is a sorry dearth, too, of those little creatures who lived there, whose homes and habits have changed through unnatural migration to the woods.

'I wonder how Clever Cousin Charlie has felt at this de-secration.'

'Who is Clever Cousin Charlie?' asked Duggy. 'Does he live in Ashdon or Glemsford?'

'He lives here in Shudy Camps in that Constable Pink bungalow near the church. Come on, we'll go and see him.' Charlie was out.

'Why call him "clever"?'

'Because he is very clever. He built his own bungalow; he repairs any kind of machinery, including aircraft engines, radio-sets and mouse-traps. He also makes dogs.'

'Makes dogs! How can anyone make a dog?'

'I'll show you. Come on!'

I led him just inside a small copse standing just off narrow Broad Street, and introduced him to Clever Cousin Charlie's dog: one he had made as a lad with his old shut-knife from a shrub of blackthorn. Only the family knew about it for it could not be seen from Broad Street. Charlie had created the dog while waiting for a pony-cart to take him to work. Each morning he had snipped away at the blackthorn until he had turned it into a terrier. Duggy was delighted, but I was not. Already saddened by the hacking-down of trees and hedgerows, I noticed with consternation the bull-dozer. It stood at Charlie's Copse, its cruel steel jaws agape as if eager to raze the copse, the next one on the ravaging list. Although we called it Charlie's Copse, this clever cousin did not own it. Other cousins did, the family of Haylocks, all first-class farmers who owned most of the land in that area. To them I was distantly related, but the family relationship, though distant, was far closer than the financial – they were farm-owning millionaires!

I was so upset by the desecration that I wished to get back home and write a stiff letter or two to my distant cousins. When I did arrive home a letter awaited me. Bearing the Haverhill postmark, it came from a rich Haylock cousin, asking if I would be the after-dinner speaker at The Rose and Crown Hotel, Haverhill, where the Young Farmers were soon to have their annual feast.

My thinking cap must be put on, thought I to myself. So I remembered a condemnation made by a Suffolk parson way back in the 1830s. Learning that some local builder and landowner wished to fell some of his oaks the vicar of Bredfield complained to our Suffolk poet, Edward Fitzgerald, 'How scandalously they misuse the globe!' Farmers have been perpetrating the practice ever since, but are not wholly to blame. Modern machines work best over wide tracts of land, so farmers want to use every square inch of their many acres, but any farmer or landlord with an iota of responsibility to our countryside could, and should, exclude the rooting up and hacking down of important trees and hedges.

I was in two minds about speaking to well-fed millionaires, country cousins or not; but I am so pleased that I did.

On the night the Young Farmers swarmed like hornets for the big eat. To my delight many Haylocks were present. I thanked them for an excellent dinner, and began. . . .

'Young farmers, old farmers, Ladies and Gentlemen, lend me your ears. I'm here to tick you off, not to praise you. When I returned from Norfolk last week, via Shudy Camps, I noticed with regret that our hedges have been hacked and our trees felled. Copses I had known as a boy had vanished. Worse still, a dirty great bull-dozer was drawn up for action alongside my Clever Cousin Charlie's copse. May God rot the socks of all the Haylocks if they root up Cousin Charlie's terrier!'

Possibly because the 'terrier' was tethered and permanently kennelled inside the copse, few, if any, knew what I had been blethering about. I explained how Charlie had snipped it into creation before Young Farmers were invented. All went well. It was a wonderful evening. They were good folk, good farmers and they all loved the land. There was a wonderful sequel. Some time later I was returning from Norwich again. We had lunch at Ipswich and Duggy was at the wheel.

'Let's go via Shudy Camps,' said Duggy. 'Your Clever Cousin might be in.'

We arrived, Charlie was out, but there was a note at the back door. 'EGGS LAID WHILE YOU WAIT'.

I looked toward narrow Broad Street. Charlie's copse had disappeared but something was there. Not a copse, not a bull-dozer. We drove towards it. A lump came to my throat and my eyes misted. Complete with blackthorn pedestal and a newly-planted blackthorn hedging to keep the Siberian wind off him, Clever Cousin Charlie's Terrier was intact.

From time to time flowers are placed near him. By whom, and for why no one knows. 'Hats off to the Haylocks!'

A second letter had some Suffolk significance, for Glorious Glemsford burst into the act. I was informed from Horse Guards that Her Majesty The Queen required my presence at Windsor on that important occasion when the Blues and Royals were to be presented with a new Guidon (Regimental Colour).

The previous presentation had been made fifty years earlier by her grandfather, the late King George V, Colonel-in-Chief of the Royal Dragoons. This was at Rushmoor Arena, Aldershot. When The Royals formed up in 'hollow square', in Review Order to receive the new Colour I formed up with them, for I was in the regimental band. The band was mounted and behind our wonderful drum-horse Coronet, the sole survivor of six Hanoverian Creams and a sight to behold when dressed for Ceremonials and bearing our priceless silver kettle drums. Lining Rushmoor Arena as cavalry escort, sitting stiffly to attention with swords at the 'carry' were our cavalry comrades of the 1st Cavalry Brigade, 'the Shiners', 10th Royal Hussars, in which the Duke of Gloucester was serving, the 13th/18th Hussars and a battery of the Royal Horse Artillery.

For me, at the age of sixteen, it was a never-to-be-forgotten spectacle and proud experience. Little did I think that fifty years later that splendour would be repeated. On that hot June day in 1924 our old faded Colour, with all its ancient battle honours, was trooped, and later put into safe keeping in the Royal Garrison Church, Aldershot.

How beautiful were our horses! We toasted them, sang for them; and because we freely intermingled in bars and messes without rank discrimination we toasted everything in cavalry sight. Old Comrades toasted the 'rookies' and vice-versa. Officers toasted 'Other Ranks' and vice-versa . . . we sang the old cavalry songs . . .

> Look at the horses, bloody great horses
> And that box, all lined with lead;
> All your relations, howling like bastards;
> Ain't it grand to be bloody-well dead!

Much-medalled Old Comrades could not be restrained from singing their favourite . . .

> Wrap me up in my old stable jacket
> And say a poor bastard lies low;
> Then six Royal Dragoons will soon carry me
> To that place where the best soldiers go.

Coronet our drum-horse did not live to attend the Windsor presentation. Only twelve of the 'soldiers' of Rushmoor were on parade at Windsor. Just one dozen from over three hundred who had been present and correct fifty years before. Major 'Spud' Lewis from Abergavenny, who had enlisted with me in 1924 and served fifty years in the Royals, formed us up in two columns of six. Her Majesty and HRH Prince Philip gave us each a swift inspection but a long, understanding chat. None of us will forget!

On my right was a semi-familiar face to which I could not put a name. He spoke with a rich Scottish accent.

'Where in Scotland do you live, you whisky-swigging, caber-hurling haggis-basher?'

'There's a village in Suffolk where I'm told you were born, Spike Mays. *Glemsford!*'

You could have knocked me down with a Chieftain tank! We had served in various stations in Egypt, India and Europe. We had both been wounded; but Andrew Marshall from Glasgow had left the Royals, was commissioned in a Scottish regiment before settling down (and getting civilized, as I told him) in Glorious Glemsford. He was elected to the Council and raised thousands of pounds for a new village hall, but now, alas, he is dead.

Major Spud Lewis and I were there at Glemsford for the clarion call of the trumpeters of the Blues and Royals, as it scared rooks from behind the church in which I was christened. They split not a note as they sounded Last Post and Reveille.

Clever Cousin's blackthorn terrier and the sound of a fellow soldier's farewell had intensified the pulling powers of the magnet. One last look at the church . . . a click of the heels for Andy!

The sands of time were running out for our thirty-year stay in Middlesex. Just a few quick trips to Steeple Bumpstead to tie up the legal knots required for bungalow purchase – like paying cash to the former owner and thus by-passing cunning agents who wished to enrich themselves. And thus enabling us to say 'Hello' to future neighbours before we said our goodbyes to neighbours of the past. On a blazing June day (in Hayes) we moved to Steeple Bumpstead where snow was dressing the

trees and painting Church Fields with a lily-white carpet. Poor
Vera was in agony with a severe attack of what had been
diagnosed as acute sciatica. With son John, who had emerged
from Welsh Wales to help, Vera travelled by train to Audley
End Junction. They finished their trip by Premier Travel
coach, arriving at our new home at half-past four precisely. I
arrived long before them, in a delivery van, and was busily
yanking out our bits and pieces when they arrived. Already I
had made a new friend, for we stopped at Steeple Bumpstead's
Fox and Hounds for a snifter.

The landlord did not look the part. He appeared to be
vocationally maladjusted. But when I told him the object of
my exercise he did a Christian thing.

'Welcome to this lovely village,' he said. 'Have a pint on
me!'

Little did he know that I had been in this neck of the woods
before the Great War. Little did I know that he was Brian
Surtees, who with his charming wife who now helped him in
the village pub, had once collected a world title in ballroom
dancing – before they began teaching the stuff on the *Queen
Elizabeth*.

We had returned to Anglia. We had a new home. A small
attractive bungalow with a small concrete garden, on which
stood a large concrete dog kennel, a new greenhouse and a new
garage.

We had no dogs. We had no flowers, plants or vegetables.
We had no motor car.

But the welcome was there. We could 'feel' it – in the land
of the high horizon.

When I say that I live in Steeple Bumpstead some people
laugh. One said it was a music-hall joke like Much-Binding-in-
the-Marsh, that I was pulling his leg. There are some divers
spellings: Steeple ad Turrin (at the tower), Bumsted Parva
(Little), Bumsted, Bummested and Bumsteda. The last syllable
of the name (sted) is Saxon. The latest spelling is considered
to be a vulgarism because a letter 'p' was added, but our wise
forefathers said that Steeple Bumpstead was the best possible
name and spelling because it told the truth and meant 'a place
or station among sweet smelling flowers'. There were luxuriant

meadows, patches of woodland, flowers, hedgerows, trees and the beautiful foliage of the park lands of Bendish, Bower Hall, Garlands and Moyns. Much of that beauty remains. Two parishes in Essex bear the name Bumpstead; the other is Helions and is smaller than Steeple and stands in the hundred of Freshwell. Both are in a picturesque valley, only two miles apart on the borders of Suffolk and Cambridgeshire. Both have good roads today and once had a good rail system providing access from Haverhill to Sturmer, Birdbrook and Castle Hedingham. It was axed by Beeching, but used to run as the delightful Colne Valley Line to the terminus at Marks Tey. Within this narrow circle of villages many trades were represented. Steeple Bumpstead boasted over ninety trades and ninety deep wells. Most of the villages were self-supporting. Agriculture was the main industry and women often worked on the fields with their men, especially in haysel and harvest. There were lots of sheep and cattle, for the Bumpsteads were blessed with good pasture land.

Way back in the reign of Edward the Confessor the parish was owned by Queen Edith and thirteen Freemen. At the time of the Doomsday survey it was in divided possession of the Peerage: William de Warren, Eustace, Earl of Boulogne, and Alan, son of the Earl of Bretagne. Much later we had another Edith of some renown. In our ancient parish church of Saint Mary the Virgin can be seen a tablet over which controversy still breaks out between patriots and know-alls of military history: all because of the wording.

In Memoriam
NURSE CAVELL
murdered at Brussels OCT. 12. 1915.
Some time a WORSHIPPER in this Church.
W.E.D. Langdale, Vicar.

'We know the Germans killed her, but she worn't murdered. She got shot because she wor a spy.' Petitions have been drawn up asking for 'murdered' to be removed and 'shot' substituted, but Edith Cavell's name lives on.

3

In Sickness and in Health

Vera's condition had worsened. The slightest move gave her agony but she wished not to see a doctor . . . 'It's lifting those heavy tea chests full of your books, I'll take a rest.'

Being bedbound was doubly distressing. The pains of whatever ailed her were trifling compared to the agony of unappeased curiosity. She wondered what the other rooms looked like since I had unpacked boxes and bunged the contents with masterly mal-distribution all over the place. She was static. Her soft bed made her worse, so I bedded her down on our studio couch which I padded with a brace of scaffold planks, then put her on a diet of pain-killing tablets used by vets on war horses. She was difficult to comfort after I tried to cheer her by suggesting hers was an affliction of convenience . . . 'You are malingering. Dodging the column and swinging the hammer when I could do with an extra pair of hands.'

Despite her pain she was glad to be in Steeple Bumpstead, mainly because of the extreme kindness of the villagers. Their visits and real concern were positively manifested by presents of sweet-peas and roses; bottles of home-made wine, various cakes, custards and pastries; not forgetting a most unusual rabbit packed in cellophane, all mortuary-stiff from a deep freezer. Bunny had been placed in cold storage for a cheese and wine party cum auction to raise funds for our senior citizens.

Personal research revealed that seventeen rabbits had been shot by community-conscious Major Noel Corry, of Gun House: a badly crippled ex-officer of the Royal Lincolnshire Regiment. He shot 'em, chopped 'em up, poked 'em into cellophane coffins before auctioning 'em, and delivered 'em door to door. Incidentally, in case a gamekeeper should take note, the regimental nickname of the Royal Lincolnshire Regiment, the 10th of Foot, is 'The Poachers' and their quick march 'The Lincolnshire Poacher'.

I had a mind to send our rabbit to Dr Christiaan Barnard, the heart transplanter, or to our local vet for autopsy. Buckshee Bunny had only three legs, but four kidneys. 'Rum owd conies in Steeple Bumpstead,' I thought.

One of our first callers was the village policeman, who stood six foot four inches in his issue socks, weighed twenty stone and measured a good yard from nipple to nipple. He was blessed with East Anglian wit and humour. He came from a large family in Ashdon: the Smiths. I had been at school with his mother Hilda who was a big strong girl with lovely, shiny, raven-black hair which she wore plaited into a pair of pigtails tied with big bows of blue ribbon. The boys used to pull 'em and swing on 'em, then she would land them a first-class clout on the ear which knocked them flying. After marriage Hilda became Mrs Marks and on 5th August 1933 she produced a son destined to become our village copper. So, twenty-six years my junior, he and I share the same birthday date. I knew his mother, but had never clapped eyes on her son. He knew my mother and had never clapped eyes on me. He was christened Kenneth.

Kenneth came to see us. He put a long pair of legs well over the top of the gate of our iron fence (other folk have to open the gate!) and stomped in.

'Welcome to Steeple Bumpstead!' said Ken . . . 'Can I do anything to help? Not because you are new in the village and that Vera is ill, it's on account of your mother. When I was the paper boy in Ashdon and used to deliver her paper she always gave me a slice of bread and jam, now and again a penny – which she couldn't rightly afford – and one day she gave me a whole tanner, on my birthday. I shall never forget her. Now then, Mr Mays, if you ever want a night's kip you just come to me. You'll have the best bloody dungeon in Essex!' We have been firm friends ever since.

Relaxing on scaffold planks did not diminish Vera's pain. After two days she reached the conclusion that some illnesses are as obstinate as Welsh women and cannot be wished away like East Anglian gipsy folk wish away warts.

'Please get the doctor. Phone him!'

Presently two young people arrived. They were locums standing in for the village doctor, Robert Fleming, son of Sir Alexander of penicillin fame. The female was Welsh and cheered Vera considerably as they yapped away in their own lingo. They handed over pain-killers to tide her over and said, 'Dr Fleming will be in surgery tomorrow.'

'Tomorrow' was a Tuesday, the day that PC Kenneth Marks had advised as the best day for me to visit the doctor. 'He likes to see the sick men early in the week. Pensioners and layabouts like you who have nothing to do. Workers go at the weekend.'

I attended, to find the drive bristling with perambulators and the surgery jam-packed with women and children.

'Have you come for medicine? He don't see men on Tuesday mornin's, it's women only.' Jeanie looked surprised.

'Ken Marks told me to come, the policeman.'

She chuckled, others laughed, and continued. 'That's jest like him, he were a-pullin' your leg. Only women an' babies!'

I scuttled out, glad to escape a pregnancy test, and telephoned after surgery. In twenty minutes Robert Fleming had disrobed Vera, prodded her in peculiar places and made his diagnosis.

'It is not sciatica, Mrs Mays, but rheumatoid arthritis. You will go to Addenbrooke's Hospital for examination by the consultant, Mr Murley.'

Two months passed before Murley could operate and Vera was bedbound and in great pain. Fortunately I was a reasonably good cook, housekeeper and nurse, so we coped. After putting on the vegetables I would sometimes pop to The Red Lion for a pre-luncheon pint. I returned one day to find Vera stark naked with Fleming holding her, trying to get her to take a step or two, for she could not walk. I spotted his tie . . .

'Dr Fleming, sir, you are improperly dressed. Why are you wearing that tie? It is the tie of the Royal Dragoons.'

'I know that. I used to be the medical officer of that regiment. How did you know it was the Royals' tie?'

'Because I served in the Royals for twelve years, that's why!'

Vera chipped in. 'He has written a book about the Royals, have you read it?'

'No! Have you got one?'

I handed him a copy of *Fall Out the Officers* and he read the first sentence: 'It was on the 17th of March, 1924, that I joined the band of the Royal Dragoons at the age of sixteen.'

'Well I'm damned!' said Dr Robert Fleming. 'That is the day I was born.'

Since then we have been great friends. Each St Patrick's Day I send him a copy of *The Blue and Royal*, our regimental journal, and a birthday card smothered with shamrock. I also invite his attention to the nominal roll given in each issue which enables him to keep count of the many Royal Dragoons who are still alive despite his doctoring.

He tended Vera well until her operation, when Mr Murley got out his tool kit. He hacked out her arthritic hip and replaced it with a Charnley, a plastic affair which, unlike Welsh bones, works painlessly for ever. Vera's health underwent a remarkable change. In fourteen days she walked without a wince. Pain left her eyes and the old light returned. Dr Robert Fleming has earned our eternal gratitude. He is one of nature's gentlemen, a doctor of understanding who goes far beyond the requirements of the Hippocratic Oath in his care and concern for the old and sick of a scattered practice. He has cured me of a frozen shoulder, a grievous affliction which compelled me to drink left-handed, and partly of bronchitis.

'You smoke too much,' said he.

'You smoke,' said I.

'I know. But why don't you smoke cigarettes with a low tar content, like mine.' He fished out a sickly-looking yellow packet to offer me one. It was empty. He smoked one of mine, Capstan's full strength. I am so glad that Vera is better. She does most of the gardening and is getting a dab hand at painting and decorating.

Flowers now abound around our bungalow, with lawnlets and verges trim and thick with clover. We have lots of flowers throughout the seasons, all grown from our flower seed. Vera is Officer i/c Geraniums. My cuttings were placed in the special compost of John Innes to root in the warmth of our heated greenhouse. Vera's cuttings were bunged into bowls and chamber-pots filled with ordinary garden soil and placed on the top of my piano. Her cuttings prospered; mine perished.

Our concrete kennel is now a well-equipped workshop. I make toys for village children and children in hospital; dovecotes for doves, kennels for dogs and trellis-work for village fêtes and Royal British Legion raffles – all from off-cuts scrounged from carpenters and builders. Knives, scissors and shears are sharpened on my lathe in return for new laid eggs, fresh fruit, vegetables and the occasional haircut. We don't need a motor car. Our garage has become a store for Vera's paints and brushes – and for me a refuge to which I pop out when the gossips pop in. I have christened it The Jawbone Retreat. We could not be happier!

4

Praying and Preying

Another visitor during Vera's illness also became a firm friend: our parson who has been described as a 'Man of God who's a Man of the People'. Not without justification.

The Reverend Eric Wheeler was the vicar of the two parishes of Steeple and Helions Bumpstead for twenty-five years. After forty-eight years in the clergy, at the age of sixty-nine, Eric earned just over £38 a week. He described himself as 'an extroverted infiltrator' because he came to our village from Yorkshire. His two sons, then aged seven and nine, had earned choral scholarships to Cambridge. Their parents wished to be near them. Eric was very much a man's man, not afraid to say what he thought in or out of the pulpit, who enjoyed a drink at the local, rode to hounds (Thurlow and Puckeridge), kept a horse named Bobby and a golden labrador beloved by every villager. The dog was called Toby on weekdays and Tobias on Sundays.

Eric wrote to me when he learned from my brother that I was going to live in his parish and asked me to meet him in a Haverhill pub. In one revealing half-hour I learned that we had much in common, particularly a love of horses. Not only had he been a wheelwright, carpenter and a farrier (he used to shoe his horse Bobby 'hot' or 'cold' after making the shoes), during the Second World War he had been a Padre in the Royal Air Force, but what pleased me most was that he had been a cavalryman as well, having served for a time in the Lancashire Yeomanry. He had read my book *Last Post* and asked me to recite for him the poem written by Captain Julian Grenfell who died in action, in the springtime of 1915. Julian Grenfell was a Royal Dragoon, his poem is called 'Into Battle' . . . I recited it for him.

The naked earth is warm with spring,
  And with green grass and bursting trees
Leans to the sun's gaze glorying,
  And quivers in the sunny breeze;
And life is colour and warmth and light,
  And a striving evermore for these;
And he is dead who will not fight;
  And who dies fighting has increase.

In dreary, doubtful waiting hours,
  Before the brazen frenzy starts,
The horses show him nobler powers;
  O patient eyes, courageous hearts!

The thundering line of battle stands,
  And in the air Death moans and sings:
But Day shall clasp him with strong hands,
  And Night shall fold him in soft wings.

We looked at each other, with misted eyes. Not a word was spoken as he clasped my hand. He looked at his watch . . . 'Come on, mount and march. Back to the nunnery!'

He used to visit my wife, take her for treatment to Addenbrooke's Hospital, Cambridge, and take me to the beauty spots of dear old Suffolk, and he told me much about his life and our village.

'I have been here a long time, Spike! When I first came from Yorkshire my wife stayed behind and I rented the old gatehouse to Bower Hall, opposite the old vicarage. The vicarage was big and dilapidated. I spent a great deal of time, and some money, renovating the place. Steeple Bumpstead too was dilapidated after the last war but it was still a very rural village. Farms which today have just one man working on them had about a dozen and three or four horses as well as a tractor or two. Combines had just started to come in, but there were stooks to be seen on many a field, and stacks in many a stackyard. On virtually every farm there was a herd of cows whose milk went daily to the Milk Marketing Board. Things altered. As corn prices rose, though, and land drainage grants became

The Reverend Eric Wheeler

available, more and more cereals were grown; and within four years of my arrival there was hardly a cow left in the parish.

'The numbers working on the land have diminished as people became attracted to industry in Haverhill. Families of people who have worked on the land over generations have now turned to other industries. . . . Obviously, wages had a lot to do with that.

'The character of the village has undergone a change. There has been an influx of people from many places who commute to work, but there have been compensations. Some have bought up old and broken-down houses and repaired them.

'I am concerned about the appearance of new estates: it tends to make Steeple Bumpstead a "buying and selling population" where families come and go fairly regularly; but I am more concerned about the number of old people coming here to live, as well as for the chances of the youngsters for employment now that Haverhill has such a great unemployment problem.

'I have watched many children grow up here over the years. Thank God for the children. We have always had wonderful children. . . . There have never been any gangs or bad outbursts of trouble.'

The Reverend Wheeler was worried about housing expansion and hoped it would be halted when the new Churchfields estate was completed. He was convinced that he would be the last parson to occupy the vicarage: 'The cost to the Church Commissioners of maintaining such a large house will soon put a stop to that gallop,' said he. 'The pay of a parson is atrocious. I don't say you can't manage on it. Country parsons were once in the upper wage bracket, but the life of a parson has now become an arduous task, not the placid comfortable existence I knew when I first came here. Some parsons have four or five parishes and have become what I call "massing priests", ministers with time for services and nowt else.'

A double misfortune struck Eric. His wife had been taken off to Addenbrooke's Hospital during his own illness, a severe attack of shingles. I used to walk Toby for him and spend an hour or so with him in the evenings as he sat in front of his fire, his belly bared and covered with a red rash.

'You should see a vet,' I told him, 'or perhaps a good farrier. You've got a girth gall.'

On these occasions he would speak more seriously.

'England began to go down the drain when its men stopped going to church. Today there is either an apathy towards the Church or perhaps an inability of our people to commit themselves totally to anything of consequence. There is a lack of a deep sense of religion. Religion is dependent on a sense of life, but today that sense has departed. In its place is what I call a feeble acknowledgement of religion, but no desire to become part of it. I doubt whether people have a love of worship and of God. Some know, and others suspect, that there is a God, but like religion and worship God is outside their lives. The Church is in a barren and arid period and is bombarded with novel ideas from a fast-moving world. Before long we shall be sitting in church listening to Matins and Evensong played on cassettes. What is needed is time. The Church needs time and quiet to reflect and determine where it is heading in this crazy modern world.'

'Stop grousing, you remind me of a hymn we used to parody as we sang in Ashdon Church choir.'

'Sing it!' ordered Eric, and I did.

> We are but little choirboys meek,
> We only get three pence a week.
> The more we sing, the more we may;
> It makes no difference to our pay.

'Well done, Spike, my thesis in a nutshell! But parsons have a better song explaining why dogs sniff under each other's tail when they meet. They all went to a dog party and had to hang their fundamental orifices on hooks provided. Tragically, a fire broke out. Dogs dashed in panic and snatched the first orifice they could put paws to. More tragic was the fact that every dog snatched the wrong orifice, so they've been sniffing around ever since, hoping to track down their own. It should be sung to the tune of Hymn No. 215, *Ancient and Modern*, of course – "The Church's One Foundation". I think it is in the key of E flat.'

'Sing it!' I ordered, and he did . . .

> The dogs all held a party,
> They came from near and far.

> Some came in traps and wagons
> And two by motor car . . .

I wrote it down, about six illuminating verses, but like the dogs I lost an item of importance.

'If you sang hymns like that in church on Sunday mornings you'd get more customers and a bigger collection to help pay for the church roof,' I suggested. 'The Sunday average is seldom more than a score.'

'True, so very true, but I feel that presently I shall get more customers, as you call them.'

Eric was right. A few Sundays later he got more customers than he had bargained for. So many that we had to send for the police.

I was sitting in my usual pew for Morning Service when in trooped a horde of unwashed strangers. They occupied the first two rows of pews just under the pulpit, and seemed to be linked together by a strange device. When Eric rose to read the lesson they rose and unfurled their banner, for that is what it was, and chanted the words printed on it; the words of Hymn No. 357 . . . 'All things bright and beautiful, All creatures great and small. All things wise and wonderful, THE PARSON KILLS THEM ALL.'

The intruders were of some unspecified battalion of the Hunt Saboteurs, commanded by one Nigel Roberts who was dressed as the Devil.

Eric was profoundly distressed and angry, for he loved his pair of churches. Our congregation was larger than usual and about forty of us shouted 'OUT!' Women waved umbrellas and hymn-books, men advanced with clenched fists. Violence was avoided by Ken, the village policeman. He calmed the congregation, grabbed some banner-bearers and led them from the church as other policemen arrived. Outside our church, prancing over graves, yelling and blowing horns there were others – some carrying placards: 'THERE'S A KNAVE IN THE NAVE', 'THERE'S NOTHING SICKER THAN A HUNTING VICAR!' 'HUNTING IS A CLERICAL ERROR'.

We returned to our pews. Eric apologized to the congregation for the interruption of our service. 'These people are only cardboard heroes and will later be ashamed for committing an act against God, His Church and us, His worshippers. I am truly grateful for your support this morning.'

Eric Wheeler was thirteen and a wheelwright's apprentice when he became a fox-hunter, and just over twenty when he was ordained. When I visited him in the evenings during his severe bout of shingles he used to talk about God and also fox-hunting, but not necessarily in that order.

'There's a good bit of God in everybody, Spike. The majority don't know and that's why they cannot care. When I was a poor little curate in a Yorkshire mining village I stabled my horse behind a pub for free, and the miners used to help me with my hunting subscription. All this fuss about hunting! Hunting is a process of natural selection,' he argued. 'All things get old and decrepit, like you and me, and have to die. Foxes can be miserably poisoned, or trapped or finished off in nature's way by their predators. The cunning fox has no natural predator except the wolf. Wolves, as you know, are a bit thin on the ground in Steeple Bumpstead, so there is only the dog. Hunting is nature's way of killing off the surplus.

'I am not a man who bends Holy Scripture to his own pleasures, but I freely admit the thrill of hunting, the sound of the horn when you start up and risk your neck across the countryside. It's nectar, *nectar*! I have examined that thrill and looked deeply into my conscience about the killing. There is no mawkish sentiment when men live by slaughtering cattle by the ton. Seal-clubbing is terrible, appalling; but is it more appalling than letting them live for fishermen to rip great gaping holes in them with explosive bullets?'

'Hold you hard,' said I. 'Don't get yourself in a flummox, I'm on your side. But as you are cracking on a bit you'll have to think up a good excuse for God when you go through the pearly gates – presuming that you qualify for elevation. What will you tell him?'

'I shall tell my God that He made the world to be balanced by predatory nature. If He asks. Honestly, I don't think He will ask me – I shall tell Him that I was a predator, too, and that I killed some of His foxes.'

5

'Treacle' Bumpstead

Up the garden path we are being led. Editors of newspapers local and national have pulled wool over the eyes of innocents. Dubious information has been propagated about East Anglian treasures. People who do not know the truth about our treacle-mine should remain silent. Up with such people we should not put. So, let us defend our folklore.

In the tap-room of Steeple Bumpstead's Red Lion there was present at our table of old sweats (ancient warriors) a person who knows so much about treacle-mining that even in distant China, in Dublin's fair city, not to mention Cairo, Cork, Carrickfurgus, Clonskiltym, Queenstown, Aldershot, Bordon, Salisbury and Kinsale, he was known as Jack Treacle Read.

During the Great War, Jack left Steeple Bumpstead's National School at the age of fourteen, not brimming over with education. He began work for a shilling a week and his keep at Steeple Bumpstead's double-barrelled shop: half-grocery, half-drapery.

Jack's boss was a rum one. A dedicated bible-thumper, chapel preacher, choirmaster and shopkeeper who oversaw a prayer session combined with 'eyes-shut' Grace every morning at breakfast.

The grocery division was commanded by chargehand Harry Eldred. Charlie Sorrell was acting adjutant – at sixteen years of age – and the Other Rank, who did most of the work, Jack Read. To keep the 'rag' side untattered there had been created as a kind of curator of the cloth the charming Mistress Websdale who was assisted by a young girl. The household RHQ boasted one housekeeper and the maids, Bessie and Connie. Part of the business entailed the collection and delivery of orders from and to various cottages and smallholdings in the environs of Helions Bumpstead, Sampford and Finchingfield.

Jack drove the cart, an open affair with only a waterproof cloth to cover the merchandise. A brace of candle-lamps provided the night lighting; the horse was a weaver, wind-sucker and broke wind at both ends. Progress was slow, except on nights when Zeppelins were overhead and the horse tried hard to break into a slow jog-trot.

In the hard times of 1915 and 1916, Jack's life bristled with responsibilities. He had to clean up the shop and the warehouse, fill, clean and light oil-lamps and tote paraffin over three hundred yards from old Dare's yard. Every village necessity was sold in that shop, from paraffin to pork. They killed their own pigs, made their own sausages, pickled and smoked hams, cleaned and boiled chitterlings (pigs' bellies), and poor Jack had also to skin sixty-pound cheeses. It was a tidy hard day for a boy. He opened the shop at 7.30, lit the oil-lamps, swept the floor and put down fresh sawdust. He was scared stiff of starting off in the dark for the shop was rat- and mice-infested, like the warehouse.

Little did he realize that he had been destined to discover

North Street, Steeple Bumpstead – long ago

the treacle-mine of Steeple Bumpstead. At seven-thirty one grim, dark morning when the first daylight air-raid was perpetrated by Gothas and Taubes, Jack opened up the warehouse door, stepped over the threshold in the dark and found his off-hind foot firmly stuck.

'After a tidy effort,' says Jack, 'I yanked out my foot and found the warehouse floor ankle-deep in treacle which had escaped from a five-hundred-weight barrel. I got the old lamp and hardly dared to look. The sight that met my eyes is just as vivid fifty-eight years later as it was on that Saturday morning. Six rats were stuck in the treacle, with heads held high like swimmers doing the breast stroke.'

Jack left, and for a while worked in Suffolk at the Leiston Works where steam-engines and tractors were made. He helped to make gear-guards, and 'tin' engine-wheel spokes. Spokes had to stand in raw spirits of salts for a day. This immersion removed the scale, and then the bottoms of the spokes were washed in 'killed' spirits of salts before being dipped into a solution of boiling tin, solder and resin. The 'killing' of spirits was achieved by feeding zinc into raw spirit until it had ceased to ferment.

'The fumes half-strangled me!' said Jack. . . . 'My neck and back were covered with boils. If it happened today I would have been claiming and getting about two thousand quid in compensation!'

Up to the end of the war in 1918 he had a soldering iron and – as a sideline – mended tin kettles and pans of the women of Friston for a tanner a time. Soon he was back in Steeple Bumpstead to help in his mother's small sweetshop, before working with German prisoners-of-war in the process of tarring the flint-strewn roads.

Jack's only joy and recreation was in playing cricket for Steeple Bumpstead – on the old Camping Close directly opposite my bungalow: once undulating meadowland, but since the Egyptian invasion (from Glemsford) now cluttered with new buildings, of which Alby Westrope had something to say. . . .

'I ain't bin up this part of the village in years. Look at 'em! They corst about thutty-thousand a-piece an' look like chicken-coops!'

Jack became a fine cricketer and later played for the regimental teams in various bits of the British Empire – which was then in existence. But this is jumping the gun. When Jack's mother discovered she was about to have another child (at the age of forty-nine) he calculated there would not be a lot of space left for him. One July morning, he left Steeple Bumpstead wearing a grey check suit and a straw hat, and eventually arrived at Warley Barracks, Brentwood. Like me, at the age of sixteen, he was 'sworn in', given the King's shilling, and was accepted as potential professional soldier by the 'Flat Irons' (1st Battalion, Essex Regiment). It was there that he first indulged in the noble art of fisticuffs. Other recruits, mostly Londoners, took the micky out of swede-bashing Jack and his East Anglian twang. They had thrown his new suit and straw hat into the fireplace, after bashing holes in the titfer, when he had to strip off to take the compulsory 'rookies' bath'.

'Who did that?' demanded Jack.

'I did!' said a Lambeth lout. 'What are you going to do about it?'

Jack knocked him cold with an East Anglian clout. Later, he took up boxing in earnest, mainly because he was roused to righteous wrath by the bullying tactics of the 'townies'. Eventually he became the welterweight champion of his battalion and fought in booths and rings all over the world.

After his posting to Signals, his life became more settled, but when the battalion returned to Blighty and Bordon Camp he continued his boxing and travelled to London at weekends, to box in the Blackfriars Ring on Sunday mornings. In one bout he took one helluver hiding, and soon after his marriage he was persuaded by his wife to pack in the cauliflower-ear profession. At the end of his service with the colours he returned to civvy street and – like so many of us – to the greater battles of finding employment.

Through the good offices of a parson Jack became a postman at Braintree, but was shortly recalled to the Army as a Class A Reservist. Soon, he was whisked off to China, leaving behind his wife and small daughter. But that is not the end or even a morsel of his interesting life story. The fist that knocked them cold picked up the pen. His first book tells most of his life story in the clear language of East Anglians who have that distinctive flair for narrative.

He writes under his own name, Jack Read. His first book *Ten Years in the Life of a Country Boy*★ tells of the life of hardship, bullying and discrimination. But what shines through is courage, loyalty and tenacity; throughout his life in a country village, in the 1st Battalion of the Flat Irons (Essex) and in the Diehards (Middlesex).

Jack, like me, was one of the first of the army's wireless operators. He became an instructor in every branch of signalling: Visual, Line and Wireless. Up his busy sleeve he has another book, about his five-year stint with the Brylcreem Boys during Corporal Hitler's War. But his ten-year story ends with his second home-coming to Steeple Bumpstead – where Jack had discovered the treacle-mine. He had not made a fortune, but was able to travel by train to Haverhill, only three miles from Steeple Bumpstead, then walk in the dark; carrying his kit-bag and all his worldly goods, plus a Bombay wicker bird-cage housing an aged parrot (part-worn, but good swearer) and less than ten shillings in cash.

Yes, there were half a dozen of us at the old domino table in 'Treacle' Bumpstead's Red Lion. All living on borrowed time for we had passed the allotted span of three score years and ten. All ex-professional servicemen. A brace from the Suffolks, one from the Essex, one from the Royal Navy (the silent service) who did most of the talking, one from the Gloucesters and myself from the Cavalry.

As has always been the custom we fought old battles, licked old wounds and groused considerably about politicians and the like whose blunderings begin most of the troubles soldiers have to sort out.

'If they make wars they should fight 'em,' said Eppy, who was still badly crippled by trench foot.

'You're right, Eppy, mate,' said Tom from Maxwelton, who had served in the Gallant Forty-twa (The Black Watch, or Women from Hell). 'The warmongers dinna fight or lead as they did in the past. They wave flags and say how grand are the sojers they are sending to death.'

★ Published by New Horizon, 5 Victoria Drive, Bognor Regis.

Tom had been a violinist – until the bullets struck. Once in a while I used to play for him . . . 'Gie us Annie Laurie, Spike!'

'What about all that money we're a-spendin' on the Falklands for a few sheep an' penguins? Do you know, tergither, you can't git two pints fer a pound terday. You want two quid for one pint an' a packet o' Players. We uster hev a good night out for halfer crown. If it worn't fer the British Legion I shouldn't hev had a mite o' firin' fer Christmas. Do you know, I git my coal from owd Lowe at Thaxted. That corst more now fer a hund'ed weight that what we uster pay fer a ton. Makes yer think, don't it?'

I brought out my British Legion folder which once belonged to my father. He was the first Secretary for the Ashdon Branch. They were not called 'branches' then, but 'posts', and the British Legion was not the name of our wonderful organization, but the Comrades of War. On the outer cover of the folder, beneath the title . . . ASHDON POST – THE COMRADES OF WAR there were two portions of poetry, written in my father's lovely handwriting. . . .

> When war is at hand and danger is nigh
> God and the Soldier is always the cry.

> When war is over, and all is righted
> God is forgotten, the soldier slighted.

The second portion was a misquotation from Rabbie Burns:

> The brave, poor sojer ne'er despise
> Nor count him as a stranger.

> Remember, he's the country's stay
> In hour o' death an' danger.

I read it out then went to the old tinny piano by the door. We sang 'Tipperary' and 'There's a long, long trail a-winding' for the Great War, and 'Lili Marlene' for World War Two. We sang not a note for the farce of the Falklands. Jack Read sang not at all. He had a note-book and scribbled.

If Jack Read did not create the Steeple Bumpstead treacle-mine, he certainly discovered it, and the name 'Treacle' Bumpstead still persists, particularly in Helions Bumpstead, just two miles distant. But Jack Treacle Read did not know who put the 'Steeple' in our Bumpstead, and no one seems to know where it is.

When we were living in Helions Bumpstead just before the outbreak of the Great War we were told that 'Steeple' was far superior to old 'Helions' – possibly because it had a steeple which 'almost touched the sky'. That was why the village was given such a funny name. 'Bumpstead' was all right as a name because in Domesday it was spelt 'Bumpstede', which means 'the place where reeds grow'. Not Jack Treacle Reads, but those growing at the source of the Stour at nearby Wixoe, and round my fishpond. Local tradition in the late sixteenth century has it as 'Bumpstede at the Tower'; all because of some towering portion of Roman remains alleged to be rearing its head somewhere in the north of our parish.

D'ye know what? It ain't there no more, so nobody knows for sure. Nevertheless, one E. Fleming, a local poet, was inspired to scribble down a mite of mythology. I love it. Partly because it speaks to me like the voices of our older villagers, but more so because it was a gift from Jack Read.

It goes down very well at other villages nearby when the Steeple Bumpstead Players are often asked to recite it. . . .

> Once Steeple Bumpstead had a steeple
> Beloved by all the village people.
> It was so fine and tall and stately,
> No wonder they admired it greatly.
>
> But long ago an angry wizard
> Blew Steeple Bumpstead folk a blizzard;
> And suddenly the dust went dancing
> And hayricks in the fields went prancing.
>
> The wind set windmill sails a-whirling,
> And pots and pans and plates a-twirling;
> It struck the folk and made them scatter,
> It beat the village eggs to batter.
> It caught the farmer's wife so busy
> And round she went till she was dizzy.

It blew the thrifty, mean and lazy
Till one and all were nearly crazy;
And one and all, both dull and clever,
Cried 'Howks a-mercy! Well I never!'

But in a wink the storm departed
Far quicker than it ever started;
And everyone came out and wondered
And stood awhile and looked and pondered.
Then suddenly cried all the people
'Oh! Steeple Bumpstead, where's your steeple?'

The steeple, once so tall and splendid,
A heap of rubbish had descended.
Its weather-cock, so bright of feather,
Had fled the country all together,
And left the place no means of knowing
Whatever way the wind was blowing.

And tales were told, and heads were shaken
To see a village so forsaken.
And all because an angry wizard
Blew Steeple Bumpstead folk a blizzard.

Steeple Bumpstead is a scattered parish of about 4,000 acres, two miles south of the Suffolk town Haverhill, often mispronounced by furriners as 'Have-a-hill', 'Hay-ver-rill' and 'Halfer-ril'. True Suffolkers call it 'Haverull'. The heart of the village beats at the bottom of the valley of Bumpstead Brook, a trickling and sometimes cascading tributary of the River Stour which runs from south-west to north-east through our parish to join the main river at Wixoe. The current population of about 900 is well served with a wide range of facilities. As Bertie Willett said: 'We hain't gotter goo nowhere. Tha's all 'ere an' we don't goo shorter nawthin'!'

Perhaps the widest range of goods and services can be obtained from our village Post Office where pensions are paid, stamps are licked, letters and parcels posted. Coins about the size of a five-penny piece, all milled of edge with a hole in the centre to transform them into washers if need be, are issued by the Post Office twice a year to senior citizens. These are stamped National Transport Token and are worth ten pence towards local bus travel. But Postmaster Stanley Drapkin, who is a Justice of the Peace, a County Council expert and an accountant, can also flog tickets for theatre shows in distant London, tickets to proceed there by Premier Travel coach, or any other place in the British Isles. While you are waiting he will book you for toenail-trimming by the Saffron Walden chiropodist, a seat at Haverhill Sports Centre for boxing, swimming, indoor bowls, opera, ballet or bingo. Our branch of the Royal British Legion, which includes Helions Bumpstead, Radwinter and Hempstead, has the privilege of using his beautiful gardens for an annual fête. GPO combines a general store, grocery, tobacconist and stationers, ice-creamery, plus a wonderful sweet-shop where all the old favourites are on view in those glorious glass jars: humbugs, black-jacks, gob-stoppers, hundreds and thousands, and tiny mauve hearts smelling and tasting of lavender.

Smack opposite the Police House in Chapel Street stands Colin Clark's emporium. Colin purveys petrol and pink pa-raffin, performs radio and television services and sells and repairs all manner of electrical contrivances. Friend Colin is a whimsical one who suffers not from wit deprivation.

'I wish to buy a pencil torch,' said I to Colin.

'My vast quantity of pencil torches ran short only yesterday. What the hell do you want with a pencil torch, metty?'

'The pads on my saxophone have warped. If I put a torch down the bell I can see which pad is leaking.'

'There are two retired majors in the village. Major Corry is an expert on guns and he lives in Gun House. He has a thing to shove up and down rifle barrels!'

'I know all about it, but I wish to make music, not war!'

'Major Roberts was an Armourer in the 13th/18th Hussars. Just five doors from here. He's got things for looking up and down gun barrels. How about him?'

'I told you before, *music* not *war*!'

'Master Mays, you are making life difficult when I am doing my best,' rasped Colin in mock severity. . . . 'Do you know Linton Zoo!'

'I know where it is, but have never been there. Why?'

'You must go. You should be an inmate. Ask at the desk for Philip the Peerer.'

'Who the hell is he?'

'A highly talented gentleman and personal friend. Looks like a Bengal Lancer. Carries a long pole with a bright light at one end. Comes in handy to inspect the throats of kangaroos, giraffes and ostriches suffering tonsillitis. Good morning!'

Hayes the Undertaker was also a 'character'. One who had made wooden aircraft for the Royal Flying Corps before making wooden overcoats for the departed, told me many a tale about his eventful life – in deep, rich dialect.

'We had ninety trades in this village, and over ninety wells full of clear spring water. We never wanted for nuthin. I've bin a builder, jack-of-all-trades, you might say. Had to be. You'd never believe the jobs I've done. Bricklayer-mason, plasterer, carpenter, painter an' decorator, with a mite of plumbin' slung in fer makeweight. I were a clodhopper an' all, wukked on the land, but the wust job of the lot was bein' bottom-boy in the village sawpit. Damn grut logs, mostly oak, from Langley Wood. They hatter be sawed inter planks with a cross-cut saw. Talk about sweat! Coo! In five minutes we wor' whully drouched. The man allus stood on the top of the log, to guide. The boy hatter stand in the ditch underneath ter pull the saw down. If it rained the poor bugger would be up to his arse in water and allus covered in sawdust. I jacked that job in. . . . Towd the Master I wor' whully fed up wukkin at the bottom. Do you know, do you know what he say to me? He say, "Come you on, boy. . . . Howd you hard! There's on'y two jobs in this wicked world where a boy or man can start at the top." That's what he say. An' when I axed him what they jobs wor', do you know what he say? He say ter me, "Grave-diggin' an' well-borin'!" That's what he say!'

'What did you say to that?'

'I say, "You ain't far orf the mark, met. You ain't as daft as you look." I got the sack an' joined the Flyin' Corps!'

Although such establishments are thin on the ground in East Anglian villages, Steeple Bumpstead boasts a 'Beautique' whose doors are like those of stables, opening inwards in top and bottom halves. I should have written 'boasted'. It *was* our lovely 'Amelia Anne Beautique' until a couple of months ago.

Vivacious Barbara Randall used to lean over the bottom bit of the old stable door, put on her friendly smile and lure the boys and girls, and the men and women, into the depths of her shop and persuade them to buy the most colourful and up-to-date garments. In the evenings, when the Bumpstead Players were in full throttle, she would lean over the village hall footlights, clad in topper and tails and fishnet stockings and rasp out Cockney songs galore. Barbara has gone. So have the old stable doors. Veronica took over first, a magnificent north countrywoman who drove London buses in the Blitz, and can still drink a pint of Guinness and sing 'Annie's Song' ('You fill up my senses . . .') while licking the pants off old Charlie Portway, the ninety-four-year-old ex-copper, at cribbage. Then came John Plummer to the Beautique and transformed it into an emporium for video tapes and such. And now, guess what? For 'Beautique' read 'County Butcher'. . . . And that ancient shop, once known as The Village Stores (and Treacle-Mine) bears a better name – 'The Shopping Basket'.

As Wally Marsh said, all those years ago . . .

'Do you listen, boy. . . . If things don't alter they'll stop as they are!'

There is a restlessness among the young. Older folk are too close to the older convention into which they were born, and in which much of their lives has been passed, to feel or appreciate the restlessness of the young generation and its desire for a life more expansive than that which the village can offer. In the ten years I have lived in the village only three boys have gone to work on the land. They have never cut a furrow with a wooden plough drawn by a pair of Suffolks. Nor have they handled a horse, nor been unduly concerned about the vagaries of weather. The drudgery is gone, thank God!

Tractors are intriguing and comfortable. On their tops are miniature greenhouses made of plastic through which the drivers can see, but through which the sun shines and the rain does not pour. It helps to muffle the transistor's noises as the ploughman plunges his non-weary way to the end of the field. I sometimes wish that someone had taught me friend William F. Dooley's poetry before I began work on the land . . .

'Hodmedod' (snail)

When he wor at school th'boy Lubber wor slow;
They culled him 'owd Hodmedod' ther, as I know.
Of all o' thim stories, thet Parson once brought us,
He on'y remembered 'The Hare an' the Tortuss'.

He got away loight wen things hed ter be done
Loiker a garden ter dig, or a message tew run.
The Master he say: 'Ut's no use tellin' him;
He'll be harfen hour afore he begin.'

Wen owd Farmer Cook at his Watersoide Farm,
Went in fer a tractor, an' put in his barn,
Young Lubber he say: 'That'll dew me a treat,
All Oi gotter dew is tew set on the seat.'

Soo, he reads abowt 'ingines' along of a book,
Thin he put his best hat on an' sin Mr Cook;
An' th' Lard on'y know what young Lubber did say,
But he's droivin' that tractor tew this very day.

I have never driven a tractor and I have made up my mind
that I never will. Maybe it is because of Wuddy Smith's
condemnation when the first tractor came to the village of
Ashdon; and Place Farm (where we both were working) sold
all our wonderful horses: Jocky, Punch, Captain, Boxer and
Barney.

'Don't loike the look o' that new-fashioned owd article,' said
Wuddy, spitting tobacco juice on the tractor's bonnet. . . .
'Do you know, boy? 'Cos o' that owd thing a lot o' clever
men'll lose their jobs!'

If I am compelled to drive, hire or buy a tractor by State
Decree, or by the National Farmers' Union I need but take
about three hundred paces beyond the hawthorn-hedge bird-
sanctuary of my back-garden: our precious spot, where each
year our blackbird pair and missel-thrush partners return each
year to raise their young.

T'other side of that hedge is a veritable nest of tractors, plus
battalions of agricultural machinery of all kinds, ranging from

hay-rakes to monster combine-harvesters; not one has put its prongs in the womb of the fertile soil. All spit and polish and all brand-new, standing like Chieftain tanks at Horse Guards, or missile conveyors on the Red Square of Moscow. Yes, I am living in a nest of mechanization, once owned by John Suckling of Steeple Bumpstead, now by Cowies from God knows where, but my missel-thrush starts his dawn chorus with a Cockney accent, tinged with Yiddish.

Midway between Steeple Bumpstead and Helions Bumpstead is a fine house known as Bumpstead Hall, owned by my good friend Ron Chapman: a first-rate farmer, despite the fact that he is sorely crippled, who, when patrolling his estate on Shanks's pony, resembles a mobile human question-mark. At our local we occasionally meet for the lunchtime snifter.

'What are you hevin', Spike?'

'Half of bitter, same as you, but I don't like drinking with farmers. Next week I'll be taking the lot of you stubble-burners to court.'

'Wassup, then?'

'Plenty. When my missus was in hospital I did the washing. Hung it up to dry and in less than an hour it was three shades blacker than midnight. We've just got shot of the harvest bugs and now you're burning the straw.'

'Can't help that, now we've got combines. Only stubble left. Ain't long enough for thatching.'

'You've got nothing to thatch. No stacks for hay or straw, and as you know I used to go thatching with my father.'

'That were a long while ago, Spike. We used to grow special wheat then, with long straw, jest for thatching.'

'I know, I used to drill it, the wheat. We had two special kinds of wheat, "Little Josh" and "Yeoman".'

'That's right. Don't hev it no more. No names, jest numbers.'

'More's the pity! An old mate of mine wrote a poem about thatching, want to hear it?'

Ron left, but the words remained, in my memory. . . . Willie F. Dooley wrote them.

Young Benjamin Batchin, wen he wor a lad,
He used tew goo thatchin' alonger his dad;

What taught him tew do ut as clever as he.
(A masterly thatcher wor owd Mister B.)

But th' boy fell tew smokin' an' that dudent match
Alonger his business o' larnin' tew thatch.
The owd man he mobbed him, but that worn't no use,
Th' young wor gettin' tew big fer his boots.

Although his dad towd him, again an' again,
He wor thatchin' one day an' he set ut aflame.
He set on the ridgin' hollered like mad
'Same's a scarified pigeon,' remarked his owd dad.

'Thed shud teach him a lesson, an' give him more sense,'
The owd man went on as he leant on the fence.
'Oi 'spose by the roights Oi shud let him remain,'
But the Lard God hedd marcy, an' brought down the
    rain.

6

Retrospection

Pipe in mouth, baccy in pocket, stick in hand and hat on head, I walked off to Haverhill, Suffolk, to stay a few days with brother Leslie. Fifty-seven years earlier our whole family had been to Haverhill Gala, my father driving us in a hired pony trap. Women were gay there in new summery finery and big-brimmed straw hats all flower bedecked. They had travelled to the show from neighbouring villages in gigs, dog-carts, broughams, wagonettes, and on Shanks's pony. Candy-striped in reds, yellows, blues and greens, and shining in the strong light, huge gas-filled balloons strained on whitewashed tethering ropes; their wicker baskets filled with men and women in gay caps and silky blouses, and sacks of ballast: all ready to take off for the big race. There were hurdy-gurdies, swings, tinkers, roundabouts, clowns, coconut shies, hoop-la and hokey-pokey stalls, and bright brass bands playing at the same time but with different tunes. Horses and ponies were spruce, satin-coated and split-plait-braided with rye straw in mane and tail, and with crinkly rosettes on the brow bands and jowl studs of head-collars, all ready for the judging. There was long, lush, daisy- and buttercup-studded grass, and high hedges, higher spirits, music and laughter.

Long after dimmit light, when the sun had gone down and the smoky naphtha flares had taken over, and we had left the gala behind and were about to turn what is now known as Reuben's Corner to enter our brick and flint tied cottage home, I fancied I could still hear the song of the roundabouts. They had played one particular tune. I had learned it from boys at school in Haverhill. When I sang the Ashdon choirboys' version to my mother, just to show off, I received a swift clout of the ear. 'You wicked boy! Go and wash out your dirty mouth!'

A swift clout of the ear is a grand aid for recollection. I

still know those words and like them – and sometimes sing them. . . .

> Oh, oh, oh, my sweet Hortense,
> Got hairs on her belly like a barb-wire fence.

I sang them when I left brother Leslie's home that day when I walked from Haverhill to Ashdon to recapture the poverty, richness and vitality of my childhood; retracing my mother's steps before the Great War, when we were half-starved and she pushed brother Leslie and sister Poppy in the old pram, with me walking, to Auntie Harriett's funeral. It came back so vividly.

The barn under whose thatch we had sheltered from the jersey-soaking thunderstorm looked mothy and slatternly of thatch. There were still white-posted railings at the bottom of long steep Whiten's Mere Hill where we stole and ate a swede from a farmer's field because we had no other food. Shudy Camps Church was locked, bolted, chained and barred as if the stench from the new battery pig farm was trying forcibly to enter where humans had ceased to go. Trees and hedgerows had been felled and uprooted, leaving fields exposed to the chill wind which blows so keenly from the Urals, for there are no intervening features 'twixt the Urals and the East Anglian Heights. In Suffolk and Essex it is known as 'the lazy wind' . . . 'It's too bloody lazy to blow round you, my owd met. So the bugger blows straight through you. Makes yer whully frawn [frozen] to think onnit!'

There were no Suffolk Punches on the fields, not a pony trap on the road. I counted eighty-five motor cars on that nine miles of country road, whose drivers neither waved, spoke, smiled nor offered a lift, not that I needed the latter. Two rabbits had been ground into the tarmac by whirling wheels: one buck, one doe, two-year-olds; one hedgehog and missel-thrushes twain. 'Stormcocks' as they do say in Suffolk: the only bird that sings in the rain.

Only one pair of human feet other than mine were on those roads, although I met three people not in motor cars: near Nosterfield Farm, two young girls, one seated on her pony, the other on the seat of her bicycle, her hand in the pony's mane for towing. I wished them good day, then told the dark-haired horsewoman to press her knees more tightly to the saddle-flaps, keep her toes up and her heels down, her legs well behind the girth, and to ease and feel the reins with her thumbs up for good luck. She told me her pony's name, said I knew about horses and riding, and was my tie the Pony Club tie. I said it was, in a way. That it was the tie of the Blues and Royals. 'Have they a club in Saffron Walden, then?'

The other pair of feet was only spasmodically on the road and belonged to the new landlord of the old Bonnett public house. One who doubted if I could get a cup of tea – in the lovely old village of my boyhood.

'Pubs don't open before seven. Nearest café is in Cambridge. Good twenty mile from here. Stoppit!'

He yelled the last word to the dog whose strength was superior, and I watched the new landlord of the old pub being hoisted most uncomfortably on a semi-airborne 'walkies' by his black Alsatian.

Walking round Reuben's Corner to Brick and Stone Villa brought throat-lumpiness. Granny Ford's and ours had been knocked into one cottage. Not a speck of mud under the eaves. But when we lived there house-martins, swifts (Jacky Devils) and swallows came to see us and live with us every summer. Perhaps the farmers' doses of insecticides and herbicides have killed off the insects our birds used to feed on, I thought. Worse, they may have killed the birds before they could rear their young – or even lay their pretty eggs.

Two meadows away the old mill, Bragg's Mill, as it was often called, still stood as the landmark on the highest point of the surrounding countryside. I was so pleased. My great friend Christopher who used to live in one of the two millers' cottages in Mill Lane taught me, among many other useful things, the words of some unknown and undated poet. . . .

'Our village mill'

Above our old village there rises a hill
And right on its top is a tall wooden mill.
The sails, when the wind blows, go merrily round,
And there all the villagers' gleanings are ground.

The miller uprises full early each morn
And fills up the hoppers with ripe golden corn.
Then round goes the mill and grinds it with power
Till nothing remains but brown bran and white flour.

> Blow, winds, blow.
> That the mill may go,
> Then the jolly miller will grind our corn.
> Soon the baker will take it,
> And into bread bake it,
> And bring us new loaves
> In the early morn.

Anon.

Sixty years ago that mill pulsed with animation. On iron-clad wheels sturdy tumbrils and wagons were drawn by shire horses whose hooves punched holes in the unmade road, hauled loads of grain up the old Mill Lane which still winds from the main highway. And when the drovers arrived, Wuddy Smith, Barney Bland, Reuben Ford and Walt Stalley, all farmhands from Place Farm and Overhall Farm, Braggy the miller would be waiting for them: his face, hair, arms, clothing smothered in the life-giving dust of his trade.

Cottagers used to walk miles from distant villages with their sacks of gleanings from harvest fields to seek out Braggy. Some farmers allowed the use of their barn floors to thresh the corn gleanings with the flail. But farmers had no devices for grinding corn. Billy Bragg always gave especial attention to those small sacks, reducing their contents to good flour which retained the germ of the wheat, to be taken home to the cottage bakehouses.

There had been two such postmills in Ashdon. Some say the other one just decayed and sank into the heavy soil; and down Kate's Lane there is a circular patch of dark-green grass where it used to stand, so they do say.

Bragg's mill had been tarted up with new sweeps, fresh paint and had been shackled; locked into the direction of the prevailing wind. I could not view the mill from my favourite spot in father's wonderful garden any more. Standing on the viewing point was an ultra-modern bungalow, with every mod. con. and a shiny metal garage whose doors flash up and down to open and shut the tin box at the touch of a switch; just like slick, silent Neapolitan blinds. And on the left, where used to tower the trees of our Harvest Apple, Golden Noble, Blenheim Orange, russets and the William pear, there is hardcore and concrete.

Steventon's spring water, clearer than crystal, still trickles through the land-drain pipe, but no one hand-catches it for drinking any more, even the tied cottages are piped and tapped. We used to cart it up the flint road in galvanized buckets, and had many a sore shoulder because the hard yokes bit into the soft skin of young yokels.

An old name on a new gate brought vivid memories of the kind old bachelor Walter Stalley, a wonderful ploughman who for sixty years had worked daily at Overhall Farm with my maternal grandfather Reuben Ford. The black lettering spelt out WALT'S COTTAGE. My heart jumped. Under Walter's Blenheim Orange apple tree I had tried to become initiated into sexual activity with my golden-haired neighbour. Pretty cousin shrieked like a rabbit being 'stared out' by a stoat, raced up the path and reported me to Granny Ford. . . . 'Granee, granee!' she hollered. 'That boy Cedric jest give me a dutty owd kiss!'

Instead of the heavenly bliss I had expected (through earlier reading of *Peg's Paper*) I received a stinging clout of the ear from Granny's dwile (dish-cloth), 'Take that, you dutty young davel . . . I'll tell yer father.' And she did. Much later, after Nellie's love letter was found by Mother, I was 'took to task'.

'What's all this nonsense about girls?' Father tried hard to look severe. 'You ain't got the cradle-marks off your backside. You ain't old enough. Keep away from your cousin Ellen, she tells tales. Go and tell your mother I've just ticked you off and you're sorry. You'll hev plenty of time for gals later on!' He patted me on my shoulder, gave me a cunning old wink, and said, 'If you find one you can't tackle, bring her to me!'

Walt's Cottage had been modernized. Water gushed through titanic taps shining like gold, with letters 'H' and 'C' let into their ebony tops so that townfolk could tell the difference 'twixt hot and cold. Talk cascaded through telephones, transistor radios and television. The lady who had bought the cottage for £37,000 was one of the top brass of the United Nations Organization. She wanted peaceful weekends.

Ashdon Place Farm barn

Mother could have bought it when Walter died. She had tended him so well in his declining, so very well, that the Stalley family offered it to her for £30.

'You shall have it, Lizzie dear!' But Lizzie dear could not muster thirty shillings, so she put on her brave face. . . .

'Don't want it. That owd thatch must be fuller fleas!' Later, when they realized the state of Dear Lizzie's financial cramp, they offered her the cottage free, gratis and for nowt.

'One house is more'n enough at my age, and I never accept charity!'

I stayed for a bit outside Place Farm whose fields I had worked upon in all seasons and weathers. Twenty paces more and I was on the grass verge of the huge tithe barn wherein Barney Bland and Poddy Coote ground mangold wurzels and linseed cattle-cake. They fed the hoppers with big barn shovels and I turned the handle; getting blistered fingers, before we mixed up the lot for cattle bait. We worked like beavers and sang like choirboys because we had all been choristers and knew all the hymns in *Ancient & Modern* and most of the psalms in the Psalter, together with alternative tunes and chants. Although Poddy had been our leading choirboy at Ashdon's All Saints' Church, one who trilled in treble solo verses like 'How sweet the name of Jesus sounds to a believer's ear', his trilling terminated on the day he began to work a sixty-hour week for ten bob at Place Farm. His voice broke. Almost instantly he became (intermittently) a terrible tenor and bastard baritone.

If tenant farmer Bidwell was out of earshot Poddy would sing his bawdy bull song, usually preceded with his own harvest hymn. . . .

> All is safely gathered in,
> If it ain't, it oughter bin.
> All upon the barnyard floor,
> For the rats an' meece to gnaw.
> Come, ye thankful people, come;
> Drink up your ale and let's get home.

'Come on, all together, you lazy buggers!' Poddy would pitch a note or two and off he went. . . .

There was a bull in Derbyshire
Who had two horns of brass;
One grew out of his head sir,
The other grew out of his
Rye-dingle, Derby-dingle, Derby-dingle day!
He were the finest bull, sir,
That ever did feed on hay.

Now when this bull was young, sir,
He tried to play a trick;
He tried to jump a five-barred gate
And paralysed his
Rye-dingle, Derby-dingle, Derby-dingle day,
He were the finest bull, sir,
That ever did feed on hay.

Now when this bull was dead, sir,
He got buried at Saint Paul's,
And it took one man and a boy, sir,
To carry one of his
Rye-dingle, Derby-dingle, Derby-dingle day.
He were the finest bull, sir,
That ever did feed on hay.

The memories left me feeling deserted and alone. Only the bait-mixer left alive!

Walton's Park loomed up, the squire's mansion where I started work as boot-boy, before leaving school, and cleaned knives and poultry, fetched kindling from Home Wood in the dog cart. I lit the fires, plucked poultry, skinned rabbits and hares, fetched the mansion's drinking water from gardener Midson's spring well, tended two ponies (Big Joey and Little Tommy), and best of all learned to ride bareback: out of squire's vision, after taking the estate's post each night to Old Eason's puny post office.

My squire, Major Tansley Luddington, taught me to shoot with a .410 rifle, and one day when I had fainted through lacking a breakfast, ordered that I should have the same food for luncheon as he did: in butler Freeman's pantry, away from the other servants who might embarrass me. Major Tansley was no longer alive. A new Walton's Park has been rebuilt and is now owned by Edmund Vestey. My Walton's, that wonderful house where I first learned some of the tricks of living, had been burned down.

There was no one about. Not a flower in the verges of the 'Carsey'. Posh people called it the 'Causeway', the Estate's private road and a short cut to Bartlow Station. In late March one used to see smotherings of violets and primroses, and heard the cooings and love murmurings of the whirling white fantails who laid pecks of pinky eggs in straw between the joists of the harness-room roof. I moved on.

Those stout hedges of Holden, Thruskell's, New Lay, Old Lay and many other fields had been hacked and slashed by a tractor-borne mobile barber. Father had taught me to hedge and ditch; to make the cleanest of cuts with sharp billhooks. My pulse quickened. I felt gladdened, with a tinge of sadness. . . . Was it still there? My heart thumped, for there it was. Halfway down New Road Hill. Our gate! The gate where I told my schoolgirl sweetheart Nellie I was leaving her. Going off to be a boy soldier in the band of the Royal Dragoons.

On that gate we used to swing and sometimes kiss. It will never swing again, nor will we kiss. Time and rust have shackled those stout hinges for all time, as her love and sweetness have manacled my mind.

From one of the new council houses opposite The Bricklayer's Arms a voice rang out.

'Come yew on in, Ced. Hev a drop of Hilda's dandelion!'

General was waving from his window. His real name was Gordon Goodwin, but because there had been a 'Gordon of Khartoum' who managed to make Generalship, fellow farmhands saw no reason why 'Gordon of Ashdon' should not be similarly promoted. Ever afterwards he was called 'General'.

General had recently emerged from Addenbrooke's Hospital, Cambridge, after drastic surgery. Hilda looked very concerned.

'He can't see very well, now, but he knew your footsteps. This dandelion is five-year old! Cheers!'

'They tell me I shan't never wuk ag'in, Ced. . . . Drop more? Done me bloody share, as well you know.'

We used to work together on the fields.

'Tell me, General, how you learned to know everyone in the village by their footsteps.'

I reminded him of the dark night when I had walked up New Road Hill for the first time in nine years, two of which had been served in Egypt and five in India. And in that blackness, when I could not see a hand in front of my face, a voice rang out. It was General's. 'Goodnight, Ced. Spect yew've got a mite of leave, then.'

General chuckled and winked broadly at Hilda. 'Easy, when yew hev tew! It were like this. . . . We were a-livin' in Collier Row. Times were bloody hard. All them kids an' mother never let none on us hev a mite o' vittles till father come home from wuk. "Yar father goos owt to arn the money for food. He's the fust t'be fed. Yew'll hev to wait, the lot o' ye."

'Well, Ced, bor, we were that bloody famished, we uster set by the front door a-listenin' fer father's steps. We larned lots o' the tothers. Couldn't stop listenin' arter that.'

I walked to Collier Row. Mrs Smith was pleased to see me. She used to live next door to mother after Granny Ford died, and was a firm friend. I wanted to see the graves, and asked, if I raced up Church Hill, would I be in time for Evensong?

'Evensong, Ced, boy! They don't hev that no more. Arter-noon services now. Parson'll soon be knockin' that on the head, I reckon. O'ny three tunned up last week.'

In the old yard of The Rose and Crown Hotel, where once were held timber sales, sheep and cattle auctions, there were many motors for it was now a car park. Friend Christopher's mortar-mixing shed had become a garage with not a line of poetry on its walls. The club rooms of the Loyal Order of Ancient Shepherds and the Antediluvian Order of Buffaloes, together with Dr Palmer's old surgery had been transformed into a well-appointed restaurant with an extensive and expen-sive bill of fare. The new ex-Grenadier landlord proudly showed me his 'improvements'. He had not covered ancient papers and fabric with plastic and formica, but had painstak-ingly removed papers and thick varnishings of over two hun-dred years, to reveal old tapestries and fine carvings in the panels of the original oak. He told me that Sheddal Wood had been conveyed to the trust of the Essex Naturalists in 1969, to protect that beautiful East Anglian flower, the 'true oxlip', together with other species of wild orchid, spurge laurel, ramson (wild garlic), currant and spindle, bluebells, bugles and anemones that make the glades of the sixteen-acre wood sheer delight in springtime; where stout ash, elm and sturdy oak provide towering singing rostrums for the sweet-voiced, multi-coloured tits and warblers.

Two new Ashdonians entered the lounge. Brogue-shod, trendily-dressed, their accents were like disc jockeys' and weather reporters'. They did not understand the language of the next entrant. I did. It was music to my ears. Cyril Williams was the grandson of the late builder and village undertaker, 'Starchy' Williams, who had earned his strange nickname through his professional dealings with 'Stiffs'.

'Glad t'see ye, Ced. Pity you worn't earlier. Wally Marsh the hurdler were ninety yesterday. He'll be abed b'now!'

I sent Wally a birthday message and some baccy and felt a bit upset. From that bay window overlooking the central point of the village I could see a motor car at almost every house, but not a soul walking Crown Hill. It was not yet dark. Blinds were drawn, as though for the passing of the village I had known. Identical flickerings of light shone through the blinds, at the same time. I looked skyward for stars, almost obscured by a forest of TV aerials.

'To think that Chris and me made the first wireless set in the village!' I said to myself, and ordered a large whisky.

7

Helions

'Buster' Moore, a couple of Germanies, Thakes, Dockerills and Claydens have taken me to task. . . . Albert Andrews started it off, and I started school with him.

'They tell me you've writ about Steeple Bumpstead, Ashdon and Glemsford. Why not say a word or two about our village, the one where you started your schooling?'

To silence envious tongues and repair an abominable omission, a word shall be said about 'Helions'. Oxford dons and Cantab clots call it 'He Lions', but here we say 'Helluns', it's easier on the tongue and folk know what we're talking about.

Helions is a microcosm of a village, one which has changed less in character and population than other villages of my ken in over seventy years. I first went to school there in the autumn of 1914 because I was too frail and ill to start until I was seven. We hadn't had a lot to take to, as they say about folk on the hunger trial. I remember little of the school – which no longer exists because a village hall had been built on its old footings – except that on 5th August 1915 Mr Shaw, the village schoolmaster, gave me my first book, *Tales from Shakespeare*: a kindly present on my birthday. When I hold it the floodgates of childhood's memories gush and cascade to remind me of important events; of the time when our sleepy, poverty-stricken community erupted like a volcano.

In 1912 our East Anglian farmers were beleaguered by newly-organized land workers. From its headquarters at Fakenham in Norfolk, the Agricultural and Rural Workers' Union gained many men from Essex, who strongly defended their right to belong to a trade union. A branch was formed in Helions Bumpstead in 1913 and forty-one farm workers joined, following the pattern set in other parts of rural England.

Standard wages were thirteen shillings for a full week of sixty hours, but when time was lost in winter or wet weather, often as little as six to seven shillings a week. Out of this the men had to buy their own tools.

By January 1914 membership had increased to eighty-two out of a total of a hundred and thirty farm workers. Farmers were alarmed by the national surge to join a union, and in February four local farmers issued ultimatums.

Two at Helions Bumpstead (Copy Farm and Helions Farm) gave employees notice to quit their work and their tied cottages – unless they surrendered their union cards. The men refused, walked off the farms, and stated that they would not resume work until the farmers agreed to raise their wages by two shillings a week.

Thus fifty-odd men transformed the farmers' lockout into a strike, the precursor of the Agricultural Uprising. Union officials tried to call a meeting to settle the dispute, but the farmers declined. A number of workers evicted from their homes were accommodated in the homes of fellow workers not living in tied cottages.

A ballot was held in neighbouring villages in June 1914 and all the men voted to strike. Old-fashioned 'rough music' at midnight and dawn – the ringing of bells, blowing whistles and thumping of tin-cans – announced that the strike had been extended, for about four hundred men were now defying the farmers. This was almost ninety-five per cent of the working force of Ashdon, Birdbrook, Helions Bumpstead, Ridgewell, Steeple Bumpstead and Sturmer.

They were asking sixteen shillings a week for labourers, eighteen to twenty shillings for stockmen, twenty shillings for horse-keepers; one half-day off a week and holidays for Christmas Day, Good Friday and Bank Holidays; overtime at sixpence an hour, harvest rates at eight pounds for four weeks and six shillings a day after four weeks; and for all tied cottages to be held on a three-month tenancy.

It was haysel, time for the hay harvest. The long green grass that had been cut was rotting in its swathes; the uncut grass seared and died where it had grown. Still the farmers were stubborn: they would rather lose a precious hay crop than meet the workers' representatives, even though they were strongly recommended to do so by the Bishop of Chelmsford. The workers were obdurate. Eight men were arrested for taking a blackleg's pitchfork to prevent him harvesting the hay. Two were fined two pounds with costs, the rest one pound with costs, and all elected to serve a month's imprisonment rather than allow fines to be paid from union funds.

Then they marched like Grenadiers to Saffron Walden police station to give themselves up – escorted by two hundred fellow labourers carrying hay rakes, pitchforks and red flags.

Demonstrations continued, daily mass meetings were held at which agitators exhorted the strikers to acts of violence. Hay ricks were fired, wagons overturned and agricultural implements placed across highways and by-ways to impede farmers and police. Not one gate in the parish was left un-broken. Animals broke fences and strayed to feed on gardens and allotments. Untended arable land became fouled with weeds; docks and thistles bristled in cornfields and what little harvest there was had to be gathered under police protection. Arrests were made and a number of strikers served sentences in the old gaol in Cambridge.

On 3rd August 1914, two days before my seventh birthday, and only one day before Britain declared war on Germany, the Farmers' Federation gave way to the strikers and agreed to reinstate them on a basic wage of fifteen shillings; keeping men at work in inclement weather, and paying harvestmen eight pounds for four weeks.

The strikers hailed this as an outstanding victory, but it was a long, long time before the Helions Bumpstead land recovered; for 'War was at hand and danger was nigh, and God and the Soldier became the great cry'.

The most positive signs were to be seen in the three village pubs, The Marquis of Granby, The Peg and Whistle and The Three Horse Shoes. Old men of the village produced Union Jacks and posters of Lord Kitchener pointing his finger. They urged the young men to enlist by croaking 1914's 'Top of the Pops'. The children loved it and would join in, for they could swear without getting a clip of the ear. . . .

> Come on and join, come on and join;
> Come on and join Lord Kitchener's Army.

Ten bob a week, plenty grub to eat,
Bloody great boots make blisters on yer feet!

And from *Rule Britannia* they warbled . . . 'Britons never, *never*, *never* shall be slaves,' and they believed it, despite the fact that throughout each minute of their working lives they had been exploited slaves of the farmers. There were exceptions. Some Helions Bumpstead farmers had been very kind to us.

The village has changed but little. Just one pub, The Three Horse Shoes, to which I was invited one evening. My Steeple Bumpstead copper drove me there.

'Come on, Spike, let's nip down to the "Shoes" for a gargle of Abbot ale, the stuff they should pump into politicians to make the buggers human. More'n likely you'll see a couple of your old mates you went to school with and hear a few yarns.'

There were quite a few there. Even some survivors of the 'Uprising' who once ploughed behind a pair of Suffolks and had drawn furrows as straight as a die with the old wooden plough. They had the same names as those on the War Memorial. Even though two world wars had been fought since I last saw two of them they called to mind things I had forgotten.

'Got any stair rods for sale, Spike? Charlie Jacobs could do with a few. He's a rich farmer now, at Clare. They've bought a new stair carpet, but can't get brass rods!'

'Charlie reckons it was you who started him on a life of crime. He's never got over it, but poor owd Siddell Germany's bin dead years.'

'You went to school alonger Blanche Chapman, Ron Chapman's sister. Ron's farming at Bumpstead Hall, but Blanche got wed. She's Mrs Stevens now, got a farm at Wixoe. Prettiest gal round here for miles! You got a hiding off the policeman for nicking them stair rods. Don't you remember?'

I had forgotten all about that. It happened in the first year of the 1914–1918 war. All the Helions's boys made wooden swords and guns, German helmets from brown paper and English tin hats from white paper. We had battles and wars, pretended we were English and German spies, and the girls put on white armbands with red crosses and made themselves into Red Cross nurses. We used to sing the song about bloody great boots making blisters on our feet, and another to let the grown-ups of Helions into a great secret . . . Kaiser Bill was a coward. . . .

At the cross, at the cross
Where the Kaiser lost his hoss
And the eagle on his hat got blew away.
He was eatin' currant buns, till he heard the English guns,
Then the wicked owd bugger ran away.

It was Charlie Jacobs who lured me into a life of crime, not the other way round. Charlie worn't satisfied with a wooden sword like the other boys, he allus wanted to be different. He persuaded me to pinch mother's brass stair rods. There were twelve in all, but we only wanted one a-piece to polish up and stick in our belts for swords and be superior to the wooden sword warriors. Charlie hit on a plan to get shot of the unwanted ten. We flogged them to Germany the Higgler, the man who brought round eggs, bought rats' tails, rabbit skins, moleskins and all kinds of metal junk.

We had a tanner for ten rods and two paper windmills on sticks that would not rotate unless the boys held the stick in front of their bellies and ran like the wind.

The wooden sword brigade reported us to the schoolmaster. The schoolmaster reported us to the policeman. The policeman reported us to our parents. We received a hiding from each, and a ticking off from one parson and one Sunday school teacher. I only got a windmill. Charlie got the other, plus the tanner from Germany, which he kept. Mother's hiding stung most. The copper only gave us clips of the ear with his cape. We didn't notice much difference in schoolmaster Shaw's hiding from those we had received in the past.

Although I had forgotten all about it I could remember the other things, the deprivation and belittling of my mother. We had stale bread, it was one farthing cheaper than new bread. We had skimmed milk, one farthing cheaper than fresh. Mother gleaned beans at sixpence a bushel, and picked stones off the fields for less. We spoke of those things, and the meanness of the farmers, who have now mended their ways. They never paid men enough to live on until enforced by law. I well

remember the strike. Uncle Will was 'standard-bearer' and
carried the red flag; and there was an old poem which the union
representatives used to recite in The Three Horse Shoes. . . .

> Says the master to me, 'Is it true? I am told
> Your name on the book of the union's enrolled.
> I never allow that a workman of mine,
> With wicked disturbers of peace should combine.'

Oh, yes! their ways have been mended, thank God! I went
to a sing-song with the Young Farmers, those young chaps
who sing for us at the Pensioners' Party once a year; and also
raise funds for the needy by carol-singing. These are the young
men who work for England and paint their slogans – not on
the walls of concrete cities – but deep in the fields with their
ploughs.

8

Harking Back'ards and Forrards

Long before 2LO pumped radio programmes into East Anglian cottages, children created their own entertainment. We made our own toys. These homemade toys were legion, effective and ingenious. Whistles were made from the tenderest branches of willow and ash; pop-guns from the hollow-stemmed elder. Pea-shooters were also made of elder, plus a steel-spring 'busk' – stolen from mother's corsets or granny's stays.

From the stems of sheep's parsley were made the water-pistols and syringes. The sap-filled hollow stems of this green plant would be cut into half-inch lengths to form ammunition for a primitive gun: a pliant stick, pointed at one end. The 'bullet' would be stuck on the point. When the stick was pulled back and then released the bullet would fly off swiftly and 'hopefully' land on the neck of the enemy: like a schoolteacher or a promenading parson. Intriguing wind instruments which gave out a blaring note were also made from parsley stalks. By making an incision in a six-inch length, and bending it in a certain way while blowing down one end, various notes and tunes could be played – if one could stand the taste of the mouthpiece. When parsley stalks had died and dried out we called them 'cixies'. From them ingenious watermills would be made that turned merrily over the surface of a ditch in spate. Invariably the 'miller' would go home wet-seated, wet-footed, but happy.

Girls kept to their home-made spinning tops, stilt-walking, parading and dressing dolls and teddy-bears, hop-scotch, and 'touch'. Most of their outdoor activities centred on skipping to various jingles . . .

> Tinker, tailor, soldier, sailor,
> Rich man, poor man, beggar-man, thief.

Horse and carriage for my marriage,
Wheelbarrow, pony-cart, haycart, tumbril.
Silk and satin, cotton and rags.

We were great riddlers and had posers like: 'What goes up when the rain comes down?' Answer: 'An umbrella!'

I was leaning on a five-barred gate one night in April not so long ago. All great philosophers lean on gates, and I harked back to another riddle of long ago. . . .

Question: 'Where was Moses when the light went out?'
Answer: 'In the dark!'

I suppose I thought back to that one because several times in that week a motley throng of Steeple Bumpsteaders were put in the dark. Some of them are known as the Steeple Bumpstead Players. Queer owd lot, really: they put on plays, farces, comedies and Old Time Music Hall evenings for bowls clubs, darts clubs, old men and maidens, young men and children. They flit from village hall to village hall, and from pub to pub to dish out a mite of good cheer, and have been so successful that their engagement book remains filled, sometimes for a year in advance. On these two nights in April we had to split forces. The 'Actors' put on an excellent farce, *Widows are Dangerous* by June Garland; but while the drama group were trying hard not to dismember their lines in Steeple Bumpstead Village Hall, our Music Hall wizards beetled off to Littlebury, near Saffron Walden, to put on a show for their football club, which included old-time songs, monologues, duologues and triologues, and musical noises from the Steeple Guitar Group with lovely Dolly Woods doing her first-rate best on the piano.

Dolly had a drawback one night. She did not like the moth-eaten piano in one village hall. A couple of strings were missing, the keyboard was badly chipped and out of tune with itself, and one of its legs fell off when Dolly raised the lid to bash off some dust. She was assured that the piano would be tuned and in order for the opening night, and was told: 'We're getting a new leg for it. It's that old dog. He fancied that leg, an' he's bin a-peein' on it for months!'

We finished our Music Hall bit at Littlebury smack on time and hastened back to Steeple Bumpstead's Red Lion, where an extension of licence had been granted to enable Eddy (Bowler) Blake to throw our villagers a house-warming party. With lots of good home-made 'vittels' to eat, and more than enough drink and oceans of song, it was a very good party. Then, if not by an Act of God, and more likely the fault of Eastern Electrics, the lights went out. Plunged into inky blackness we continued in song until the saloon was lit by candles. We stopped some song in mid-verse and by some miracle of country wit, all started up with 'Just a song at twilight, when the lights are low'!

It should be made known that the Steeple Bumpstead Players is not the only group in this vicinity. All the villages are at it. On a night in the same week when we were not at it, those in Stambourne were. Their artistes kindly invited us over to see an extremely well-played comedy by David Kirk, *Love Locked Out*. One scene depicted the antics, or withdrawal tactics of married ladies who had gone on strike. *Love Blacked Out* would perhaps have been a better title. Just as the ladies were beginning to feel love-deprived and had voted to restore relationships, another Act of God intruded. The gals were about to resume boudoir duty in Scene IV – with the lines 'Let's put out the lights, dear; a lot of people will be retiring early tonight' – when there came an ear-splitting thunder-clap. Lights flickered, lights dipped, lights went out. The Stambourne Players carried on undeterred – illuminated by the light of torches scrounged from the audience.

What most impressed me was the capacity of our villagers to improvise and give such rattling good performances, with all that time required for learning and rehearsing, for such a puny fee. They made their own costumes, lighting and sets. All under the most trying circumstances. I learned later that most of the Stambourne Players had something in common with our bunch. They had been at it for only a couple of years.

Old Charlie Farrant – known as The Spy – who leaned on gates, watched everybody, eavesdropped and gossiped, used to tell about old characters who brought light to the village, before their own lights were extinguished – some, since I have 'returned'.

Miss Christie, God bless her! She was profoundly grief-stricken when Hunt Saboteurs violated 'her' church. Her hymn-singing voice was Annie Laurie-ish (low and sweet), but she had been the first to confront them, waving her umbrella and ordering them out. Our church was packed for her funeral.

Mark Barnes did not attend church overmuch. Perhaps he was too tired and ill: he had been a farm labourer in the village for sixty-nine years. Our church was packed for his send-off.

Another light, now extinguished, was Sir Peter Kirk, MP, who has gone to a better Common Market. We shall miss him, and remember him as a man who worked, perhaps died, for a very great cause . . . European Unity. There was not standing room in our church!

Five-barred gates made from English oak can last more than the average man's lifetime, and it was good to lean on one and have a natter with 'Charlie The Spy', on whom I had not clapped eyes for over sixty years. We spoke of our own ages, the age of the gate and of the craft and skill of the man who had made our leaning post.

Harry Wright was the estate carpenter at Walton's Park, Ashdon, when I was a houseboy there. Harry used to tell me about the superiority of wood over metal, that it was 'alive', not dead and cold like steel and iron. He liked best to work with oak, and taught me to plane it with 'jacks' and 'smoothers', how to dab it with cotton-wool dipped in linseed-oil to 'fetch up the grain' to 'see the beauty of it'. He taught me how to sharpen 'chippies' pencils' to stiletto-like points: those oval ones called 'chippies' carbons' – not with a shut-knife, but with a two-inch razor-sharp chisel – without breaking the lead. His white overall pocket used to bristle with pencils and rulers. He was in great demand. In his repairs to wagons and tumbrils – the splicing of their shafts, the making of ladders and other such rough carpentry – Harry's work was never a millimetre out. In the finer work, the restoration of mansions and cottages alike, and the making of household furniture, his work was perfection. He once repaired the whole of the windsweeps of Ashdon windmill, which have been more recently replaced.

Five years ago I received a letter from Harry Wright's daughter, to remind me of other aspects of her father's skill . . .

'I can just remember my father repairing the sails of Ashdon Mill. He took great pride in that work. He liked best to work in oak, then, he said, his work would outlast him. He built this house (in 1948). It has oak doors inside and outside, and an oak staircase.

'I have an oak-cased grandfather clock which he made with a carving of Father Time on the front, and the bolt is a carved mouse running up the clock. There is an oak prayer desk in Little Abington Church which he made and carved. When my sister and I were children he used to make us wooden toys, dolls, diabolo tops and spinning tops on his lathe. He even made caravans.

'He would be pleased to know that you have remembered what he told you about tools and wood, but he died in 1965. We put him to rest in an oak coffin, with oak furniture, and on his last journey he passed through the heavy oak churchyard gate which he had made and hung.

'Do not forget the men who used to make the wooden sheep-fold hurdles for our Mill Meadow. They do not use them now, but use a wide wire mesh which they call pig wire. It is as ugly as it sounds. . . .'

So we spoke by our five-barred gate, of Harry and other craftsmen who worked in wood; of the three Marsh brothers, James, Nipper and Walt, who carried on a flourishing trade and were famous as hurdlemakers, until the outbreak of the Great War.

In winter Walt would be off to the woods and hedgerows to find the best ash saplings, for ash was used exclusively in making five-barred hurdles. After hewing the poles and transporting them to his cottage yard, he cut them into lengths for 'riving' – by cunning use of the 'throw', a heavy nine-inch blade of great strength which looked like a massive opened cut-throat razor. The blade was hammered into the end-grain of the pole to be rived, then by sheer strength of the forearm the cleavage was continued until the pole was split into two equal parts.

Demand for hurdles diminished as farmers sold their flocks. War disrupted everything, and the farmer became his own shepherd when the men went off to war. Walter returned from Flanders to become a labourer on the land. He was ninety when I last saw him sitting on the wall opposite The Rose and

Crown, the old gossiping point for women when they came to the pump for water. We had no tapped supply in those days! His short blackened clay pipe gurgled with a moist dottle and was all but empty. We bought him tobacco. He lit up, sighed and spoke. . . .

'Glad t' see y'boy. Thassa fact! Things ain't what they wor. Got metal "hardles" now. Reckon if I see another ten year they'll be hevving metal sheep an' all!'

As we were leaning and reminiscing Charlie introduced a personal note. . . . 'Remember when we were out on the fields "bud-scarin'"' at a penny a day? Well, I've still got that set of they owd clappers made by Harry Wright. Not the sort we had for swingin' but the sort he made for rattlin'. Do you know, met, the farmer reckoned I were a better bud-scarer than you. You were prettier'n me; that's why the owd rooks an' starlin's uster fly orf at fust sight o' me. There were more to it, though. I were methodical. Each day I finished my bud-scarin' I uster put a stick up where I left orf. Then I'd know zactly where t'start nex' mornin'!'

We had heard it all before, but once Charlie got going he took some stopping, and off he went with a couple more of his 'tallish tales' as he called them, not forgetting his oft-repeated apocryphal, or hypothetical hit . . .

'Man come up t'me. I wor wukkin' on the headlands. He say t'me, he say, "Now, young master, tell me where's t'other Ashdon Mill? I've bin towd there were a couple on 'em!"'

'So I say t'he, I say, "There uster be two, owd metty, but Dusty had to hev one on 'em pulled down. They reckoned there worn't enuff wind t'drive the pair!"'

Comedy continued when I got home. I could see that PC Marks was present for his Essex Panda was parked in my drive.

'This is better, I can get in and out of this!' He stood up and sat down again to prove it. Until then we had trouble in seating him in the comfort to which he had been formerly accustomed. We had only average-size armchairs into which his ample rump had to be gently squeezed. When he stood up he would take our armchair with him – and might well have kept it – had not we prised it off. Vera put a stop to this performance by buying a pair of second-hand armchairs from Pryke the scrap dealer. They were beautiful to behold. In

Walt Marsh

limed oak, tastefully upholstered, they were the sturdiest of sit-you-downs; each with a brass hook below its seat to shackle it down when seas were rough on Atlantic cruises. Rich passengers had sat in them in that first-class steamship, the *Queen Elizabeth*. Ken could mount and dismount without the aid of a shoehorn.

'Have you seen the flag on the church?' asked Ken.

'Yes, it's St George's Day!'

'I know that, but it's up there for another reason you won't know about. Do you know what, I've just christened a grown man!'

'Men don't get christened,' I said. 'Only children. Parsons do that job, not Essex coppers!'

'The parson was not present, so I did the job, mentally. On the road opposite Sturmer Red Lion. Saw an old chap picking dandelions. I stopped the car and had a word with him . . . "Don't forget, mate, I'd like a glass or two when it's ready!"' Ken chuckled loudly, and continued . . .

'It's bloody funny! He said I'd better go round to his house in five years' time, because dandelion wine was no cop until it's seen three or four birthdays. I agreed with him and asked how old he was.

'"I shall be eighty-seven next birthday, in September, if the Lord spares me!"'

'I christened the bugger right away, on St George's Day, for he's what England's all about!'

'What did you christen him?' I asked.

Ken laughed, then looked strangely serious . . . 'Great Expectations.'

9

Jubilation

Although healthy in the main, Steeple Bumpstead's villagers are prone to infection, but never admit it. When you ask how they are getting on, you receive diverse answers like 'Half tidy', 'Fair to middlin'', 'Not so dusty, well brushed' or 'One leg at a time'.

In June 1977 they all caught a tidy dose of Jubilee-itis which ran unchecked throughout Britain. We did not have my old mob, the Blues and Royals, with us: they were kept busy in London as 'Sovereign's Escort' following several ceremonial stints in Edinburgh. We did not have all the City and Windsor euphoria, like electronic beacons and firework displays as were laid on throughout the land by bonfire engineers, but I know which I preferred. . . .

Our villagers rolled up their sleeves, hung out the bunting and worked like beavers to make life gay for the old and the young. In most cottage windows there were posters hand-painted with red, white and blue edges. In every cottage letter-box reminder posters were pushed: they were 'invitation posters', for everybody over the age of sixty was almost demanded to partake of a buckshee 'strawberry and cream Jubilee tea'. There was tea, gallons of the stuff, but we mostly washed down our strawberries and cream, our tasty well-filled sandwiches, and our red-white-and-blue meringues, with glasses of bubbling champagne.

This was on the Saturday, at Broadgates – a kind of preliminary canter for Jubilee Day. Although the posters specified 'all over sixty', not all the senior citizens were on parade: some were holiday-making, some bed-bound and ill, and also absent an unduly sensitive minority who harboured qualms about betraying their ages.

Well over eighty of us were most cordially received at

Broadgates by our hosts, Mr and Mrs Tony Foster – who dished us out with a raffle ticket apiece: a crafty device to count us as we came in to enable the helpers to count the plates and glasses required. On each guest we pinned a buttonhole wrapped in silver foil. Silver for the silver Jubilee as well as for protection; to hold more securely the pretty posies of tame and wild flowers. We sat at our tables on the spacious lawns like guests at a Sandringham Garden Party, and were waited upon hand and foot by a bevy of beautiful damsels in summery frocks – to make the eyes of the 'retired' stick out like chapel hat-pegs.

Broadgates is but one of some noble old farmhouses, once surrounded by pasture and arable lands, orchards and gardens, and other houses whose names are still music to many a villager's ear: Garlands, Upper House, Old Hall, Latchleys, Bumpstead Hall, Blois, Rylands, Wakelands, Lower House, Freezes and Claywall.

Before the First World War, the working men of the village were employed chiefly in agriculture, their wives and daughters in domestic service, or as 'finishers' to garments made by the clothing manufacturers, Gurteen, in nearby Haverhill, just over the border in Suffolk. When I was a boy at Helions Bumpstead, there was great poverty in the villages of Steeple and Helions Bumpstead; but the villagers did not worry unduly. Being self-reliant and reasonably contented folk they regarded their plight as the natural order of the day. Things have changed, thank God! Perhaps the most remarkable feature of our village is its general condition of health, which is proved by the longevity of its inhabitants. Broadgates' party was an excellent example of the fact. I calculated that the total age of those present would exceed 5,000 years, but they all looked as fit as fleas in Norfolk thatch.

Our host got himself into a problem. He wished to make a Jubilee gift to the oldest lady and gentleman present. When he politely asked who was top of the pops in age not a hand was raised. Tony thought they were reluctant to betray their immaturity. Harold Malyon, a mere stripling of seventy-eight, put Tony to rights.

'Why not have a count-down, Tony? Start at a hundred!'

Tony had only to count down to ninety-five.

Margaret Webb had all her buttons. Her eyes sparked like
forge hammerings. She gave me a kiss and promised to take
me 'bluebelling' . . . 'Up in the woods, Spike, on our own.
But not for another five years, love, then I shall have learned
a few more tricks!' Margaret had seen off a tidy few Coron-
ations, as well as a brace of Jubilees, like young Phil Barnes,
who, at eighty-four years, became the sole survivor of the Great
War when Porky Eppy died. Phil was an Old Contemptible
who wore the old gongs 'Pip, Squeak and Wilfred'. Both said
that 'young Elizabeth' was the best queen they'd ever had, as
did others present; but I was saddened when two old lads of
the soil told me that this Jubilee Day was very important to
them. They had never tasted champagne before. And then I
knew what John Masefield meant in his poem 'The Land
Workers' . . .

> Long since, in England's pleasant lands,
> I used to see the farming hands.
> I need but shut my eyes and fast
> There comes a picture of the past,
> Of men and women, long since dead,
> Who battled with the earth for bread
> (A daily bread they might but taste)
> For Folly and his doll to waste.

So, on that Jubilee Day our village held its celebration on
the lush grass of Church Fields and Camping Close. History
has it that Roman Legions had camped there before our
British Legion caravan. Romans knew a trick or two about site
selection, but I doubt if it looked more beautiful in their time.
It is a tranquil place almost surrounded by trees; an undulating
meadow-land dappled with buttercups and daisies. Bordered
by the village church and a brace of good village pubs it is the
centre-point of the village.

On Jubilee Day the meadows were thick with a crop of
human beings of all ages, mostly children. At noon the green-
fingered fraternity judged flower arrangements in church and
chapel. Two hours later 'the procession' assembled in North
Crescent, before marching off in slow time behind the Haverhill Salvation Army Band to the Camping Close for a united

service – Church of England, Baptists, Wesleyans, Non-Conformists, the lot!

The Reverend Eric Wheeler conducted the service. There was more singing than spouting, and how delightful it was to sing in the open air those hymns beloved by country-folk, Nos 166 and 379 (*Ancient and Modern*) – 'All people that on earth do dwell' and 'Now thank we all our God, With hearts and hands and voices'. Eric read a short lesson, gave an even shorter address and said, 'We will now sing a hymn *with* our children – and *for* our children!' It came from the *Children's Book*, such simple but meaningful words:

> Let us with a gladsome mind,
> Praise the Lord for He is kind;
> For His mercies still endure,
> Ever faithful, ever sure.

'God save our gracious queen' finished the service. As we moved off for the gaieties of Jubilation my companion – one who had served in the Welsh Guards – gave me a dig in the ribs. He sounded a bit choky.

'I saw the service in Saint Paul's this morning, on the box, with all the pomp and circumstance. It can't beat this, mate. What would old England be without its villages?'

The Law Courts should have been present to see real judges in action: they were swarming like hornets to judge decorated floats, decorated children and decorated adults, some stone-cold sober! There were sports galore: sack races, egg-and-spoon races, egg-slice races and three-legged races. While all this dashing about was in progress young gentlemen indulged in six-a-side, three-legged football. There were fifty-yard dashes, eighty-yard dashes and mixed tugs-of-war. Most were for the children – those too young to have attended the village disco for teenagers the evening before.

Then in our brand-new school a hundred and eighty children sat down for a tea provided by the villagers. 'What a blow-out!' said young Paul Godsmark. 'I went in twice. I told them I had had one lot, but they didn't care. Know what they said: "Why not have two lots?" and I did!' That worn't bad going! And this I know, for I had one lot. Each child had three sausages, several sandwiches, sundry cakes and pastries, a packet of chocolate, the inevitable bag of crisps – and the lovely children of an East Anglian country village washed down their bait with Yankee Coca-Cola. After prize-giving, every child in the village was given a Jubilee mug and a newly minted fifty pence piece – by our kindly Les Humphries.

Later, in darkness after adult jubilation in The Red Lion, I wandered home across Church Fields in thought. Perhaps it was the Abbot ale that made me surmise that it wouldn't be all that difficult to make every day a Jubilee Day.

10

Snobbery

For over sixty years, my grandfather, Reuben Ford, was employed by the Haggar family at Overhall Farm in Ashdon. He was the Reuben of *Reuben's Corner*, my first book, and shortly after it was published I received a letter from a Jack Overhill of Cambridge, who was intrigued by the similarity of his name and Overhall Farm and was convinced that it had been derived from it. We met, and became firm friends.

Jack's father was born in Haverhill in 1863 and was taught shoemaking by his father. For a time he lived at Castle Camps, then, in his late twenties, he moved to Cambridge to become a journeyman boot- and shoe-maker for bespoke shops. He worked hard but his production was not confined to footwear. He sired thirteen children, six boys (Jack was one) and seven girls. Jack was born before me: in 1903. His parents separated when he was five, and he was brought up by his father, with whom he lived alone from the age of eleven.

The industrious Jack performed six jobs out of school hours, thirty-five hours a week for three shillings a week. He won a scholarship to the Cambridge Higher Grade School, left school at fourteen to learn his father's trade, when he should have stayed until he was fifteen, but the home fire had to be kept burning.

For ten years he learned shoe-making, but also attended night school for three years without missing a lesson. The old learning bug had bitten deep, for he also learned Pitman's shorthand, typing, book-keeping, English and commercial arithmetic. Like his father, he was no dawdler in the matrimonial stakes, getting wed at the ripe old age of twenty (on two pounds per week) and producing a son and daughter. At the same age he took a shorthand teacher's diploma, became a clerk for seven years and then a bookmaker. But this was merely the 'beginning'.

As an external student of London University he graduated as B.Sc.(Econ.), became a teacher of shorthand and typing at Cambridgeshire Village Colleges, and a Lecturer in Economics at the Cambridge College of Arts and Technology. Jack has made a good sixty broadcasts, his fiftieth, 'The First Twenty Years of my Life', was broadcast twice by the Third Programme and the Home Service. No mean accomplishment, for it was unscripted and took just one hour. It was included in *Good Talk*, the first anthology from BBC Radio: my friend, the old snob (shoe-repairer) rubbing shoulders and matching wits with Sir Bernard Lovell, Professor A. J. Ayer, Sir Gavin de Beer, FRS and our East Anglian friend and fellow author René Cutforth – who helped to promote the sales of margarine for Kangarooland.

Now over eighty Jack is as straight as a beanpole, fit as a thatch flea and busier than overworked beavers. I reckon it's due to the waters of the Granta. Each morning, at seven o'clock, he has been taking a header into that river, swimming like an otter for at least half an hour – over a period of fifty-five years! He does it when the Granta is frawn, and breaks the ice to get in . . . Ugh!

Against all kinds of people, with every kind of stroke, he has won every sort of swimming cup and kind of medal. I wish not to enlarge upon these aquatic antics, and shudder at the thought. The object of this exercise is to invite attention to the literary qualities of this remarkable gentleman which overlong have been overlooked.

Jack has written thirty books of which twenty-seven remain unpublished. He soldiers on, totally absorbed in writing the last and fifteenth volume of 'The Cash Chronicles'. All are beautifully typed and bound, a meticulous, detailed account of our region: a work of love, an intimate social document of great significance. His first novel was a tale about Cambridge undergraduates, which was hailed by the then editor of *The Cambridge Evening News*: 'Over sixty novels have been written about Cambridge University, all by University men. This first book by a townsman completely licks the pants off the lot [or something like that!] and Jack Overhill was an elementary schoolboy!' Two of his books are in my shelves: *The Snob* and *The Miller of Trumpington*. I like *The Snob* best, because I know the locality and characters. Rejected by twenty publishers, David George wrote in *Tribune*: 'It is the best book of our working class in print.'

'You must see my Uncle Will's snob-shop,' said I when Jack one day took me in his car to Ashdon. Willy (Geezer) Ford lived down Halt Lane. My mother's younger and favourite brother was village cobbler and had his shop in a tiny cottage opposite farrier Bill Smith's smithy along the Saffron Walden road. Before Geezer set up shop, and after Harry Smith died, Bob Matthews served the whole parish as 'the' cobbler. Some called him 'Pablo Bob', we never found out why. He was short, slight and his dark close-set eyes were quite startling behind his iron-rimmed spectacles. He moved in jerks, like a wood pigeon, when he moved to his work or to his rented house at the junction of Radwinter Road and Crown Hill which is now the village Post Office.

Bob made boots for land-workers when they could afford a pair. Hobnailed boots were sold in both the village stores but they had not the quality of Bob's handmade boots. He made them to last for several years, strong and completely waterproof, and before handing them over he would soak them in neat's-foot oil to make them soft and pliable. He made his waxed thread for stitching, using a strong double lockstitch, and we who bought them knew well the advantages Bob's boots had over 'they owd shop jobs'. We were often over our ankles in water and mud in the fields. There were no rubber boots, but Wellingtons made of leather were to be bought, though land-workers could not afford them, and were mainly worn by coachmen or riders.

Most of his work consisted of repairs, replacing a pair of clump soles, renewing hobnails, toe and heel tips, patching uppers, or reinforcing seams with new stitching. There was not enough work for him and he was glad to turn his hand to casual farm work, then cobble in the evening. Village lads would congregate in his shop and play practical jokes on him. If he fastened the door to keep them out they would climb up the roof, bung a slate over the stovepipe and smoke him out.

Uncle Bill (Geezer) received vocational training as a cobbler;

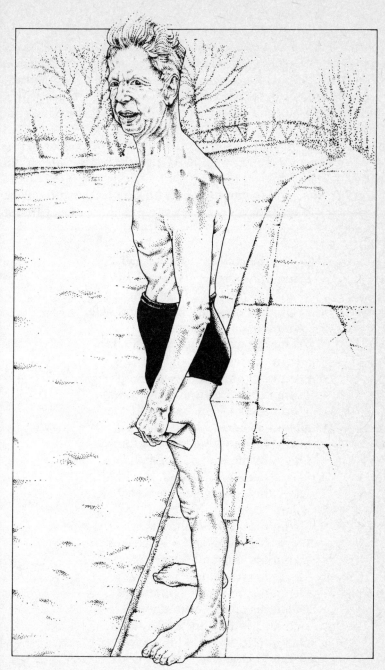

80-year-old Jack Overhill ready for his daily plunge

he had been badly wounded in the Great War and could hardly walk. He persevered and became a first-class snob and no mean comedian, much to the daily delight of our village schoolgirls who blew him kisses, asked him to tell them funny stories, accused him of living on nails (he always kept brads in his mouth when putting on soles), and always addressed him as 'Fordy, dear'.

'What you got fer dinner terday then, Fordy, dear?' The answer was always the same: ''Arf a brick, a few nails an' no taters.'

Long ago an anonymous bard laid a curse on the village cobbler. Jack and I have both tried to check the source, without success.

> Damn the cobbler, and his awl
> Damn his hammer, wax and all;
> Damn his pincers and his knife,
> Damn his half-starved kids and wife.
> Damn his hob-iron and his last,
> Damn the welts he don't make fast.
> Damn the heel-iron and the tips,
> Damn the brads a-tween his lips.
> Damn the hobnails and the screws,
> Damn the lot – his boots and shoes.
> Damn his laces, leather thongs,
> Damn his fire-irons and his tongs.
> Damn his bench and smoky lamp,
> Damn his walls, all stained with damp.
> Damn his stove what stands askew,
> Damn his sooty chimbley, tew.
> Damn his wax-end and his stitches,
> Damn his apron and his britches.
> Damn his rasp and leather file,
> Damn his jar of neat's-foot ile.
> Damn his inks and leather dyes
> Damn his crafty squinkin' eyes.
> Damn his punch for eyelet holes,
> Damn his uppers and his soles.
> Damn his lump o' blackin' cake,
> Damn his smudge he fare to make.

Damn his ink-horn and his pen,
Damn his dusky-smellin' den.
Damn his lapstone and his leather,
Damn and blast him altogether!

11

Merry Molins

Four days before the sixty-ninth anniversary of my birth in 'Little Egypt' and a hundred and forty-one days after the sixty-ninth anniversary of 'old' Bertie Willett who was born in Steeple Bumpstead, Bertie did a Christian thing.

In the richest and ripest rural lingo he hollered to me in the bar of The Red Lion.

'Hey, Spike! Come up the green tonight, we're havvin' a roll-up. It ain't a match, jest practice. If you ain't played afore we'll larn ye.'

I said I was not interested in old men's games, and certainly not in one that requires people to kneel down on bits of rubber like Moslem prayer-mats before aiming huge hunks of brown wood at a little white bit.

'When I was in the cavalry in Lahore, the capital city of the Punjab, we used to play games with a bit of wood. We didn't kneel down to it, Bertie, boy, we bashed it with a long-handled mallet from the back of a galloping horse!'

I was taken to task by bowlers present. Among them one Joseph Findlay, a genial ex-Group Captain of the junior service: an old Brylcreem Boy who was teaching new sixth-form boys at Saffron Walden High School.

'Come off it, Spike. All that Indian rubbish! It would do you the world of good and get some of that blubber off your waistline,' said the wing-and-a-prayer wallah. Anyway I accepted the challenge.

Taking great care to conform to the norms of sartorial splendour, and get as near as my wardrobe permitted to BCTO (Bowling Club Trundling Order), I donned white shirt, white pullover (three-ply cable-stitch), Household Divisional tie, grey flannel trousers, best blue blazer – with Household Divisional blazer badge – and highly polished brown brogues. At

four-thirty hours precisely I reported to Bertie Willett, who
was hurling hunks of wood behind The Red Lion – on Greene
King's bowling green.

'You can't come on the green like that!' bellowed Bertie.
'You orter hev bowling shoes or slippers. Can't goo on the
green with they heels!'

'I have slippers at home. I'll go and get them, but I've got
no balls.'

'*Balls!*' bellowed Bertie. 'Yew don't call 'em balls, yew call
'em *woods!*'

A fairish bit of time was required to learn the language,
which varied from village to village. In Suffolk the little white
bit was called 'cot'; in parts of Essex 'jack'. You could take
too much green, or not enough. On the right line, or the left;
one could be too heavy or too light, thin or thick; and to add
another complication one could play on the left hand with the
right hand, and on the right with the left. I used to try
to fathom these bowling peculiarities by sticking to cavalry
terminology – off-side and near-side, and soon I was asked to
play in matches.

One fine day I was promoted to 'skip' . . . Officer in Charge
of one rink of the 'B' team. We bowled the pants off Haverhill's
ex-Servicemen's team and were promptly promoted to the 'A'
team. I was elated, ego-inflated and boastful. I proclaimed that
I was one of the best and wished to perpetuate the practice;
adding that the cost of woods was prohibitive. In pubs without
Bumpstead I appealed to ancient, played-out players, who
might have bunged their woods into some museum or other,
to think of me. News of my woodlessness leaked. My telephone
rang. I learned that a lovely lady wished to see me. That if I
went to her Colchester home it would not do me a mite of
mischief.

PC Kenneth Marks drove me to Colchester, to the lovely
house of the lovelier lady.

'I have always enjoyed your books and articles, Mr Mays.
So did my brother. Please accept these!'

She handed me a brown leather bag containing woods,
slippers and a measuring device . . . once the property of her
deceased brother who had been a dab hand at the game – a
cup winner in County Championships. . . . My gratitude is

beyond description, for I can modestly declare that I have trundled those beautiful woods on the well-kept greens of many a delightful East Anglian village and township. My circle of friends has increased beyond expectation. My horizon has widened and my faith in human nature has been restored. . . . All because I am a member of the 'Ace of Clubs' and have trundled my gift woods at Castle Camps, Birdbrook, Cavendish, Clare, Radwinter, Linton, Thaxted, Castle Hedingham, Stoke by Clare, Saffron Walden and, by no means least, at Little Egypt (Glemsford) where I was born in 1907 and whose skilled bowlers have won cups galore.

We have played 'friendly matches' in Peterborough and King's Lynn whose teams have also been our guests at Steeple Bumpstead. All of these have been days and nights to remember when most of the community have turned out to give support, food, drink and unbelievable cordiality. My once highly polished brogues and I have parted company: so friendly were the festivities after a 'friendly' at King's Lynn that I forgot to change from bowling shoes to polished brogues, and left them in a Norfolk Club House. I am told that they are on their way back to me, in the boot of a car owned by a person in Haverhill. I hope the car owner gives them a rub over now and again. He's had lots of time – he's had 'em for two years!

So keen did I become about this bowling racket that I sometimes took morning strolls to the rinks to watch our groundsmen tarting them up: weeding, sanding, levelling, rolling and cutting were performed without payment by our three stalwarts, Jack Bacon, Denis (Buster) Moore and Pete Findlay – son of the wing-and-a-prayer merchant. My mentor Bertie Willett also took a hand. Between them they kept the greens in pretty good lick. In May 1980 they redoubled their efforts, became almost frantic, frenetic. The Top Brass of Essex Bowling had sent down spies from Girlings and Crittall Silver End. I caught them in their acts, both of the blighters!

They carried weights and measures, a gadget like a theodolite and pointed poles. They were like Joseph and wore coats of many colours, all badge-bedecked. Old Hermann Goering and Bernard Montgomery between them had not so many decorations as these prodding personalities: their lapels were plastered with them and every blazer pocket. Never before in the fields of outdoor bowling have so many decorations been worn by so few!

As they prodded they jabbered. . . . My trained ears detected the lilt of the Welsh, so I addressed them in that language, to their surprise, and before The Red Lion had closed I got to know them quite well. Both came from South Wales. One had been a Bandsman in the South Wales Borderers. He was a saxophonist. The other had trilled as a tenor in the Treorchy Male Voice Choir. In The Red Lion we had a singing festival, but before we yodelled I discovered the origin of the Silver End Bowling Club. They came from Cwmbran during the depression of the 1930s, settled in Essex and formed their own Silver End Club. Inevitably, they had to sing about it.

Before they departed they taught me their bowling anthem. One which has to be warbled to the melody of the Welsh Hymn 'Uw pob un' and to the English Hymn 'Who is on the Lord's side, who will serve the King?' The author of the parody is Jack Millership, who (so rightly) claims the words embody the feeling existing between all clubs, and probably the whole bowling world. The words were sent to me by Ernie Edwards the spying saxophonist who, with his Silver End accomplices, had been sent down to discover if Steeple Bumpstead's green was suitable for County Play. I informed them that if they did not give an answer in the affirmative, I would have their intestines for suspenders, or something like that.

Our green was judged to be 'highly suitable' by the Arch Druids of Silver End who later brought their team to play on it. When the 'socialites' were trundling nicely after one exciting game, members of both teams were caught 'full frame' by a press photographer while in 'full throttle' – singing their bowling song . . .

Bowling is our pleasure, bowling our delight!
Joy beyond all measure every day and night.
When the woods are rolling up and down the green
A happier band of people nowhere can be seen.

Chorus

Bowling, bowling, bowling,
Let this song ascend
Till the great Archangel Skipper calls 'Last End'.

There are 'Leads' in plenty, number 'Twos' abound;
'Thirds' are bowling gentry, 'Skips' can still be found.
When they are together, what a happy throng.
Sunshine or foul weather they will sing this song . . .

Chorus

If the game's a tough one – thing's not going well,
Show them you're a sport, son; then you're doing swell.
Just to win is pointless, play the game's the thing;
If you do you'll bless the day you learned to sing . . .

Chorus

We sang before, during and after matches. No one ever
got breathalized or gaoled. One illustrious member, a former
'Singles' champion – whose father had helped Charlie Clay-
den's father move our bits and pieces from Helions Bumpstead
to Ashdon on a handcart all those years ago, will not sing with
us again.

Anne Moore telephoned me, just after dawn.

'Spike, whatever shall I do? Denis is dead!'

Denis (Buster) Moore went out like a light with a heart
attack. There was only standing room in the church when we
put him down. He's in good company in the churchyard with
another good bowler, Eric Wheeler. We have a cup in his
honour. Bowlers come to play for it every year – from all over
East Anglia.

We call it the 'Buster Moore Trophy'.

We still sing about the day we went to Molins. For over a week
that tune was seldom out of my head, and it was all on account
of Derek. We were 'invited' to Molins, not 'commanded'; but
genial and efficient Derek with accomplice Brian Haylock

made a courteous, civil invitation sound like a direct order from
Field-Marshal Monty. Pamphlets were dished out; portions of
paper were puggled through post-boxes and telephones trilled.
Every child one met on road, field, path or mede delivered the
same message . . . 'Don't forget! We go to Molins on Sunday!'
I was reminded of the old army manoeuvres held in the East
Anglian Heights in 1912 when the London Scottish in Hodden
Grey kilts fired their musketry course at targets erected in the
chalk pit at the bottom of Chalk Hill, near Saffron Walden. The
air rang with rifle shots, bugle calls and stentorian commands.

I half-expected to see pinned up in the post-office Steeple
Bumpstead's Part II Orders: 'The Club will parade in FCBO
(First Class Bowling Order) on Church Field's Parade Green
at 1200 hours. Woods, jacks, score-boards, measurers and
mats must be cleaned before vehicle entry. Haversack rations
must be mouse-proof. Dogs must be led, and wives shoved.
Umpires will be stationed at strategic points; wearing armbands, carrying flags and thunder-flashes. They will judge the
conflict and their decisions will be final.'

The Molins War was not a bit like that. Non-militant,
non-political and non-sectarian, it was a simple sporting event
between community-conscious countryfolk: the bowlers of
Bumpstead versus the maestroes of Molins. For weeks the
Bumpsteaders had been preparing their ammunition. Woods
were freed from rust, dust and woodworm. Measuring devices
were freed from harvest bugs and elasticity. Beermats had been
'borrowed' from pubs elsewhere to wipe from our superior
woods the inferior soil of inferior bowling clubs. Blazers had
been dry-cleaned, county badges burnished, trousers pressed
to razor-edge creases. Vera made me rush for church at eleven
o'clock to hear a new parson who normally sermonized about
celestial pastures, not bowling greens, until twelve-fifteen. 'Cut
the bread! There's lovely Welsh ham. I'll mix eggs and curry!'
Church-bells sprinkled eleven crochets over the village as I
jammed the egg and curry lot into a super-hygienic plastic
container whose lid would seldom keep on or come off. We
raced over Church Fields clutching to our bosoms hot curry
and boiling thermos flasks. We sat, kneeled, panted a psalm,
croaked out canticles, prayers and responses. The moment the
parson put his foot on the pulpit steps, we shuffled out. It

crossed my mind he might suspect we could not stomach another of his sermons, or were dodging the collection, or both. So, I made a financial offering to a fellow worshipper who was not proceeding to Molins, asking him to put it on the plate.

Bowlers of Molins do not live at Molins. It is the name of their factory firm who manufacture up-to-date, highly technical devices for the human race, like large STOP SMOKING signs that flash like meteors in orbit, together with coin-fed cigarette-vending machines. Only the top brass of our Committee knew for sure where we were going. Perhaps that's why we only got lost twice. The coach driver let the cat out of the bag after a swift look at his watch . . . 'I don't reckon it'll take quite a couple of hours, my beauties! We ain't stoppin' nowhere till we git to Peterborough. If you wanter water yer nags, better hev one afore we set orf!'

The trip was interesting and educational. Up front sat Basher Blake (Aircraft scientist and Wall-of-Death expert) alongside Dickie Bird from Sussex. Both were seedy and looked it, due to overnight revelry. Bird had bruised his starboard hip, Basher had broken his port arm by compound fracture. They had fallen over each other down Church Road, in the light of the harvest moon! Neither would miss Molins . . . Hellabit!

Social scientists, economists, philosophers, psychiatrists and barrack-room lawyers – of which every East Anglian village has its quota, told us newsy items about Molins. . . . 'It is one of Britain's most go-ahead firms,' said the economist . . . 'Actually, the firm got The Queen's Award last year, for outstanding production.' 'I understand they manufacture cigarette-vending machines,' piped up the non-smoking philosopher. 'We have a high incidence of cancer in the lung as it is!'

Sweets were proffered and sucked, cigarettes were offered and puffed, gossipings were whispered and comments were made about the beauty of the countryside through which we so pleasantly were passing on this warm sunny day. After about an hour the scenery changed. Tall chimney-stacks were sighted on the off-side.

'Great brick-working here, metty. I reckon they make the world's best bricks, Flettons! The Government made 'em put up tall chimney-stacks to stop the pollution. Know why? It's on account o' the cattle. Herds of 'em up here, you'll see 'em in a minute, wholly beautiful they are, all pedigree, sheep as well, look!' And there they were, like blobs of mobile cotton-wool on a vast green blanket.

Presently we drew into the yard of a huge pub bristling with banners and crowns and christened Gildenburgh. Out poured the passengers with sandwiches at the alert position, seeking seats at the *al fresco* tables. In poured the thirsty bowling fraternity to the innards of the pub whose bars resembled Texan ranch houses. The resemblance was heightened as I entered the 'gents' to hear a stentorian command, 'Stick 'em up!'

Lo and behold! Behind me towered a nigh-on seven-foot cowboy. He wore all the authentic cowboy gear, sombrero, leather chaps, jingle-spurs, and on his gun-belt a brace of holsters, one toting a Remington 44; the other Remington was in his right hand – its muzzle stuck in my back. Peterborough was swarming with the varmints, for it was a fête day for Westerners trying to look like cowboys, and Western pop-singers trying to learn to sing. Fair play to the cowboys, they did not rob us, not one of them . . . Only the smoothie barmen, who demanded sixty pence for a pint of Abbot!

The Molins' club secretary met us at the Municipal Gardens, shook hands with all the men, kissed all the gals, then led us across the beautifully kept grounds to meet our hitherto unknown opponents – with whom we swapped Christian names and were swiftly on the best of terms. The wood-trundling soon began.

According to certain seditious commentary, Bumpstead were beating the living daylights out of the Molin tribe, on every rink, until it was time for tea. After tea, a brew which had not the appearance of being 'doctored', there came a sorry deterioration in Bumpstead play. There was no outward and visible sign that a vet could detect, but the scoring-boards took turns for the worse. No one cared two hoots.

The Molins' were a mixtie-maxtie lot, as the Scots have it. From all walks of life, in Ireland, Scotland, Wales, Germany and Austria, they quickly proved that statement of Rabbie . . . 'We're a' Jock Tanson's Bairns!' Their cordiality and welcome was truly heart-warming. After a first-class, four-course meal together, served by their kindly kitchen staff – on their day off – we sang together, danced together and raffled for prizes, and there were lots of prizes: prize-giving over we perpetuated the pleasant practices . . . music and dancing, dancing and music, dancing and yelling, dancing and shrieking, due in the main to the haggis-bashers and two new friends . . . Pip (The Chair), whose eyes moistened when our Brian (The Chair) handed him a plaque we had made in token of our appreciation, and Hamilton (The Haggis) who wore his kilt, his Hamilton tie, but had served in the Gallant Forty-two, or Women from Hell, better known to the Ministry of Defence as the 42nd of Foot (The Black Watch). 'I'll be down to Bumpstead shortly to see you, Sassenach!' said Hamilton of Hamilton. I told him that I was no Sassenach.

'That title was given to Lowland Scots, not East Anglian gentlemen,' said I.

When I was seriously ill he came to see me. I would have liked to have gone to see him when he was seriously ill. It was too late, alas! One Flower of the Forest is a' weed awae!

12

Hearts are Trumps!

Years ago, in most East Anglian villages, a public hall was built by the squire for use as a general meeting-place: for dances, receptions, lectures, and for all kinds of entertainment including concerts by the village band. Today it might appear difficult at first glance to notice any change, but there has been a revolution. Now that the old rural hierarchy has declined, the element of patronage has vanished. The new village hall and the playing-field are both democratic institutions and are handled by representative committees. Clubs and societies too numerous to mention have sprung up overnight like September mushrooms. They exist for every known (and sometimes unknown) purpose for both sexes and for the old and young; from dominoes to discos, jumble sales to Jamborees. Some schools have been changed into village halls, and where I first went to school in Helions Bumpstead, before the 1914–18 War, and was caned for taking mice to school to frighten the girls, and for swiping mother's brass stair-rods, there now stands a first-class village hall. Few of these halls are privately subsidized as in the past, but depend on membership subscriptions, supplemented by the proceeds of organized entertainments.

All this is part and parcel of the democratic development of the village, yet some of the old 'uns take a dim view of it and express their regret. Nevertheless, if the village is to survive as a living community, such changes are inevitable, but one important factor has changed hardly at all. It is perhaps the most important factor: the countryman still provides a large proportion of his own amusements. These are mostly 'homemade' and do not compete with the inferior attractions of the town; for he manages to enjoy both. I well remember a wonderful example. . . .

Harry Hutchins once farmed at Overhall Farm. He was a

very jolly soul with a zest for life and a partiality for good ale on Saffron Walden market days, and any other East Anglian town's market day he could reach with his pony and trap or motor car. Returning from Saffron Walden one night with more than one sheet in the wind Harry perceived light in the windows of the Conservative Club Hall. The Women's Institute were in the throes of an auction of odds and ends. Bull-and-china-shop fashion Harry barged in – just as Mrs F. held up an old vase.

'How much am I bid for this? Who will make me an offer?'
'Half-a-crown!' squeaked Harry.
'I am bid half-a-crown . . . Any advance on half-a-crown?'
'Five bob!' squeaked Harry.

Harry continued to bid against himself, for there were no other bidders, until the vase had made twenty-five bob. Mrs F. handed the vase over to Harry, who squinted at it, then squeaked, 'I don't like the look on it, put it up ag'in!'

The vase was put up three times. Harry bid twenty-five bob three times, then kind ladies took him home, but left the vase behind.

Partly because of these village halls our villages are surviving as 'living' communities, not as a collection of old stones; and it is in the halls that one sees and appreciates that quality of self-support and self-sufficiency that distinguishes the social life of the village, and the villager himself, and that most important element, the human element. If you don't believe it, come with me to a whist drive and put it to the test: at Linton, Castle Camps, Steeple Bumpstead, Haverhill, Keding-ton, or a number of other villages. According to the state of weather and roads, most of the whist-drivers meet at one of the halls, at least once a week, and manage to fill fifteen to twenty tables. There's nary a frown or scowl to be seen on the faces of seventy or more villagers. Most are country folk, and the women are particularly attractive. Their clear skins devoid of make-up, their strong capable hands that have tended cattle, flower-beds, tried old and new recipes for home-made wine, bottled fruit, crab-apple jelly, jams, spices, pickles and all manner of cakes and pastries are positive indicators of their diverse abilities.

The dialects differ but slightly 'twixt the villages of Suffolk,

The author

Essex and Cambridgeshire, except by pitch, lilt and rhythm, but the differences are there and if one closes one's eyes when entering a hall one can tell which county predominates among the whist-drivers. Now and again one hears old words long out of general use, to remind one of woods and weather and the dawn chorus . . .

'Had a tidy owd dag this mornin', started at dimmit light, kept on all night an' I got soused jest lookin' at it!'

'What did you ever do oo they long socks you won last week at Linton, Spike?'

'I've kept 'em for you, m'dear. I've got them with me, and after the whist drive I'm going to take you bluebelling up Langley Wood. I'll put the long socks on you there if the grass is dry!'

'Never you mind the whist, come you on now. Never let yer mother know she bred a Jibber! Wassit gonna be, Whist or Woo-in?'

I had won the booby prize, a pair of diaphanous double-barrelled stockings known as tights. The willing lady was my senior by two years.

On Monday nights Eddie Blake would drive three of us to Linton Community Hall: Greta (Ken Marks's wife), Jack Bacon and myself. Eddie was jack-of-all-trades and the village Walter Mitty. He had personally designed night-fighters for the Royal Air Force, had ridden motor-bikes on the 'wall of death', was a gardener, carpenter, engineer, painter and decorator and was distantly related to royalty. His brother-in-law warned us to take a pinch of salt with Eddie's stories, and continued . . . 'If you write down all the things he's done, and how long he spent a-doing 'em, you'll find he's getting on for four hundred and twenty-three years. Don't look too bad on it, do he?'

Jack Bacon was a Gunner in the RHA who served in India and many other stations at home and abroad and excelled at all sports. He now works for the Essex County Council and does yeoman service for our Bowls Club – and usually wins the best prizes at whist drives. I make the fourth in Eddie's car load, but there have been occasions when I have wished I was elsewhere.

Coming back to Steeple from Linton one night we heard a

mysterious ticking noise in the car. Eddie pulled up and listened. Silence reigned supreme.

'It might be a time-bomb,' I said. 'Those Irish people who play whist with us might be in the IRA!'

'Pipe down, Spike!' said Eddie the aircraft engine designer. 'I will test it!' He put his foot down. As the speed increased so did the ticking; when he slowed the ticking slowed. Inspection revealed nothing. But when we reached Steeple Bumpstead and were about to enter the hostel for our customary post whist-drive nightcap, all was revealed, the aircraft engine designer had forgotten to extract his car keys from the outer lock of his off-side front door. We tore him off several strips and told him to exercise more care in future, the landlady was calling 'Time'.

On the following Monday he jingled his car keys several times to prove that he had mended his ways and his faulty memory: but that was on the outward trip to Linton. As usual the Whist Drive ended just after ten. We stood in the cold frostiness of the night, waiting for Eddie to open up the doors; but he could not. Eddie the 'Memory Man' had locked his keys in the car. We waited in the cold until an AA expert arrived from Cambridge. He had to attend to other unfortunates and we were third in the queue. I watched him set about the opening, which took about two seconds, and I learned how easy it would be to swipe a Rolls-Royce. All one needs to open a locked door is a tiny strip of celluloid!

Apart from such minor setbacks, these are truly wonderful evenings; and the consensus of opinion runs thus . . . 'It's a damn sight better'n sittin' an' watchin' the tripe on that owd telly!'

Perhaps it is because we play 'Progressive Whist', where the winning lady moves 'up' and the losing gentleman 'down'. So at every move one meets two different people, and one feels the friendship and the sense of country community. And we talk to each other.

There are prizes galore. Top score lady, top score gent; top score lady for highest half, and highest half gent; a booby, then the inevitable raffles. Prizes run from packages of now costly groceries – a boon for the pensioner – boxes of handker-chiefs, bottles of wine and preserves. The raffle is called a

'Tombola'; a strange name which originated from soldiers in India – from the Hindi words 'You speak'.

Whether or not one wins a prize, one is sure of something of importance: a couple of hours spent in the company of good country folk; a meeting of like minds which produces always a mite for charity; a place where hearts are always trumps!

We play twenty-four hands in all. After the first dozen have been played there is a tea and biscuit break which the 'men' have christened 'Jaw Break'. All the mawthers dash off to different tables to have a good natter about things past, present and future – mostly the past – to dig up old tales and find out who did what to whom and when and why. The last time I had a natter with the ladies we spoke about doctors and nurses who had tended the sick, lame and lazy of Linton, Ashdon and Bartlow, and to my delight one Linton lady spoke words of praise about Mrs Fisher of Ashdon. She was a tiny tot of a woman, who had been widowed for many years and lived alone in a cottage on the brow of Knox Hill – and had earned herself two titles, 'Mole Kitcher' and 'Body Snatcher'. She used to deliver the village babies, usually without a doctor in attendance, hence her first title, a pseudonym for 'midwife'. Not only would she deliver the child, but for days afterwards would attend to other children of the family, run errands and do the cooking and washing until the vitality of the mother was restored. She also performed the 'Last Offices' as she called it, the laying out of the dead. We had no district nurse. The nearest doctor lived at Saffron Walden and drove five miles to his Ashdon surgery in his pony-trap. My mother's doctor, practising in Linton, was Dr William Palmer. He first came to minister to Ashdon's sick on an old bicycle. Not to be outdone by 'they posh owd doctors' from Saffron Walden he, too, bought a pony trap, then opened a surgery behind the bar of The Rose and Crown – taking Dr Gill as a partner, and attending twice weekly. Palmer was conscientious and benevolent and endeared himself to the old and ill. . . . 'A proper Christian' and a 'real genuine poor man's doctor' said the farm-workers.

A second surgery was opened at The White Horse by Dr Thelwell of Saffron Walden and when he died Dr Hepworth, another Saffron Waldener, took over. They had posh new motor cars, all beamy and searchlighty at night with acetylene headlamps. Dr Palmer tried to catch up, and hurled himself into the realm of internal combustion by lashing out on a pop-popping motor-bike. He was a big man on a puny machine and looked lugubrious and disconsolate when Saffron Waldeners overtook him in their fast cars.

Paying for treatment from their pittance of only twelve shillings a week was a great problem for farm-hands, one which was often aired in the bar behind the surgery. . . .

'If it worn't fer the cost of that owd box of cheap elm with brass handlebars, payin' for that owd hearse, the undertaker, top hats, wreaths, parson and the bloody grave-digger, I'd be better off a-dyin'. Nobody wants yer arter you've wukked yer gut out on the land!'

A local branch of the Loyal Order of Ancient Shepherds was formed. Lodge meetings were held in the club room of The Rose and Crown and subscribing members became entitled to medical attention and a few shillings a week – for a limited period. Dr Palmer was mainly responsible for treatment and the clerical work. When his partner Dr Gill returned to Ireland, Dr Palmer took a new partner, Dr Wilson. He bought a brand new motor car, all chauffeur-driven. Not even Palmer's potions could have given the villagers better health and pleasure than to see him being driven about in style, even along the narrow, flint-capped roads and lanes. This splendour was short-lived. From a travelling salesman came the story that 'Owd Palmer's bein' took over by one o' they Scottish doctors. Do you know what, metty? You'll all hetter pay fer treatment in advance!' As usual, the news carrier was right. The practice was taken over by a magnificent Scot, Dr A. M. Brown, who came to love Ashdon village as much as his patients loved him. It is a long time since he retired to a new home in Scotland which he named 'Ashdon', and now he is dead. 'A worthier candidate for wings and halo never existed' was Ashdon's opinion.

Ashdon has been fortunate in doctors, but older folk of Ashdon, and certainly some of Linton's whist-drivers, still cherish the memory of William Palmer. Not only because he used to write about the villages in *The Cambridge Chronicle* with his friend Cyril Fox. . . .

'It's all owd pills an' pellets nowadays, an' I fair rattle as I

walk arter gooin' to the surgery. Palmer's jalap were the stuff.
Brought yer strength back in no time at all!'

We still hear the story of Jasper the gamekeeper who attended Palmer's Linton surgery when he was approaching his
seventy-ninth birthday.

'Mornin' doctor! I want some jalap. My virility ain't much
cop!'

'Now, Jasper, you are getting on and should take things
easy. Sit in your armchair for an hour or two. Do a bit of
reading.'

'Hellabit! I've bin hale an' hearty all me life, but me virility
hev jest let me down. There's suffin' else. I'm paid up in the
Shepherds' Club an' I'm entitled to free jalap. Come you on!'

The doctor mixed him a tidy-sized gargle and handed it
over. 'This is very strong. Three times a day in water, after
meals. Got it!'

'Thankee, good-day to ye.'

'Just a minute . . . this virility business. You are nearly
eighty, Jasper. Tell me, as a point of medical interest, when
did you first notice this sad state of affairs?'

'Very recently doctor.'

'How recently?'

'Once last night, but twice this mornin'.'"

13

Fruitility

Some years before the Great War an experiment was conducted on the heavy farmland soil of Ashdon.

Young Roderick Charlton, fresh from college and bursting with unused wisdom, conceived the notion of growing fruit on his smallholding, Springfields, where for years cereals had been planted. Tall, thin, and studious-looking, he wore a surgical boot. First he planted apple and plum trees, then between the rows, strawberries, currants and gooseberries. While the hard fruit was being established on trees the planting and harvesting of soft fruit provided employment for women and one aging man known as 'Graggy' who lived in a cottage in Rock Lane at the bottom of the holding. 'Graggy' was a tower of strength. Between the sturdy old man of the soil and the frail young man of textbooks was a bond of respect and real affection. Both worked through every hour of daylight, and were rewarded with initial success. Bumper crops were sent off regularly to market. Had Roderick's health matched his zeal his business would have expanded, but he became ill and had to give up.

Just over the hill at Sprigg's Farm, old John Desborough, who had been keeping a crafty eye on these strange activities, followed Roderick's example. Acres of his farm which had previously grown good corn were planted with saplings of pear, plum and apple and, between the standards, long rows of strawberries.

A newcomer arrived at Springfields, Walter 'Peggy' Lawrence returned from Australia where he and his wife had built a house with their own hands. Our local builders, Walter Smith & Sons, built them a new one to the old Australian design, of which 'Starchy' Williams said, 'That look more like an owd shed than a house!' 'Starchy' was allus right. He had got his nickname through his professional dealings with 'stiffs', for 'Starchy' was our village undertaker and coffin maker. One who boasted that he only made 'strong' coffins that would last a lifetime.

But the shack was a home, for five people. One living-room, two bedrooms, it was warm and dry. When business began to pick up a kitchen and another bedroom were added.

'Peggy' Lawrence had a wooden leg, from which he derived his Ashdon nickname. A forthright character, full throttle of speech, he was held in high esteem and was renowned for cursing loudly and fearlessly at all and in all presences, and until quite recently it was not known that 'cussin' an' swearin'' had saved his life.

His flaxen-haired son Wally, with the wide grin and Australian accent, who years later became the proprietor of The Queen Victoria at Dunmow, helped his parents run the smallholding, which Peggy had christened 'Fruit Farm' (part of it has now reverted to its original name, 'Eight Acres'). Peggy was justifiably proud of his fine strawberry fields and his orchard. It was a place of back-breaking industry, but of great beauty. Seven lofty elms towered at the back, hawthorn practically surrounded it. Stallentyne Hill bounded the right flank, and in springtime a sea of apple blossom billowed to the left and down the hill. His children, seated on the five-barred gate, greeted the Thakes, Cornells and Downhams on their way to Goldstone Farm for 'tater pickin''. Later, these women were employed by Peggy to reinforce his battalion of fruit-pickers from the village: Polly Web, Beat Chapman, the Heards and many more friends of my schooldays.

Fruit farming is a dicy business, liable to disruption by the vagaries of the weather. When strawberries are in full bloom a late frost can wreak havoc. Thus it was with Peggy. One May he had seen the tell-tale signs in the sky, and prayed all night. The rich dark-green leaves of his most promising crop were capped with waxy golden-eyed blossom. But next morning, on his wife's birthday, he found the frost. Instead of blossoming life there was dark depressing death. His daughter had seen her father's tears but once before, when she was four years old, when after an accident Peggy was told that his leg had gone.

In the ruin of his crop was disaster, the beginning of the end
for this courageous man. His famous 'Lawrence Strain of
Sir Joseph Paxton' had won him high award, but now his
occupation had ended and he sold his beloved 'Eight Acres'.

When the elder Desborough died his children John and Nell
carried on the good work. The fruit acreage was vastly increased
and Sprigg's Farm became famous for huge Monarch plums,
Early Rivers and Czars, which grew in equal profusion to
the fine black damsons and succulent greengages. Strawberry
production was intensified and provided employment for
many.

Although the greater part of the farmland was under the
plough, fruit and cereal production were conducted concur-
rently and successfully until the end of the war, when the
farm came under the management of Major Bill Mallett, an
ex-paratrooper. Bill further expanded the fruit-growing area
and commanded great respect from his employees. To work
at Sprigg's Farm today is a kind of horticultural symbol of
status, as well as a means of earning a living.

'Eight Acres' (Peggy's owd place) changed hands several
times. There was neither acreage nor scope for expansion, but
the trees which were planted by young Roderick Charlton still
bear fruit in season.

Fruit-pickers have filled the places of the gleaners of my
childhood. They are gaily clad in colourful slacks and sweaters.
The talk, badinage and laughter is heard from lipsticked
mouths. Mineral water, Coca-Cola and steaming flasks of coffee
have replaced those old bottles of cold, milkless, sugarless tea.
The old regulars, like fore-woman 'Girlie' Pettitt, 'Young Em'
and Hilda, Mrs Pembroke, Nell Smith and Joyce Baker perch
happily on aluminium tripods as they lift prime Cox's Orange
Pippins from fine trees in the autumn sunshine. Tanley and
Brian with their tractor-drawn sledges load the fruit boxes.
Old 'Snack' collects buckets of ripe fruit and 'Brisk' keeps
tally. All owe their presence in the lovely orchards to two fine
men: the tall, thin bookish pioneer, and Peggy (that owd
Orstralian) – both crippled in body but not in spirit.

I went to see Wally, Peggy Lawrence's son, when he was
the proprietor of The Queen Victoria at Dunmow, our first
meeting for over fifty years. We had a whale of an evening and

I intended to pay another trip to Dunmow. Frost was not responsible for the calamity; it was fire. The Queen Victoria burned down and Wally lost a lot of money.

People were present on my first trip to tell me more about Wally's father . . .

'It happened when he were out in Orstraylor. Had suffen' wrong oo his chest. The doctor lived twenty mile away. Peggy set out to walk it, along the railway track. 'Cos there were a tidy wind a-blowin' he put up the hood of his owd duffle coat. He never heard the train what hit him, poor bugger. He were lucky, tho. On that day two trains were runnin'. Peggy heard it a-comin. He hollered, an' shruck, and swore and cussed so bloody loud that the engine-driver heard him. Peggy were very lucky. . . . If he hadn't bin a good swearer he'd hev had a wooden overcoat instead of a wooden leg!

'There worn't many about who could beat owd Peggy at swearin'. But *nobody* could beat him at growing strawberries, met!'

14

The Thirst after Righteousness

There's cryptic for you! 'Landlord dies – pub closes.'
Doubtless *The Haverhill Echo* had better things to write
about in January 1978. I was mighty distressed to learn that
my old friend the late Len Murphy, one time landlord of The
Bonnett Inn at Ashdon, had handed in his chips. He was only
sixty-two, a little Londoner: hardly tall enough to look over
the top of his bar counter as he served pints of Greene King
ale to tall and brawny farm-hands. I felt equally distressed
about the pub closure, but there was a shred of consolation in
the words that the closure was temporary, and so it was.

Brick and Stone Villa, where I lived as a farmer's boy, was
about two hundred yards from The Bonnett Inn where the
squire's and farmers' employees gathered most evenings for
warmth, drink and companionship; and once a year to give
thanks for Harvest in a 'Horkey Supper'. It was at this pub
that my grandfather Reuben Ford, who worked at Overhall
Farm just up the lane, had his own 'place', where others were
warned . . . 'You marn't sit there, metty. That's Reuben's
corner!'

Standing high above the other tied cottages of Bartlow
Hamlet, under the proprietorship of Bill Cooper – for the
brewers Greene King – the hamlet pub was our community
centre and social club and a most companionable place. We
had nary a church, chapel or shop. In winter a great fire
invariably roared up the chimney. Pokers would stand ready
and waiting for the 'Beer Warmers' to perform their winter
ritual. With their backs shielded from draughts by the tall
backs of oak settles they would start the drill by 'ordering
up'. . . .

'Let's hev a quart and a pinch, then!'
The performance would begin with the following procedure:

Stand frothing quart pot by the fire.
From 'pinch' (nutmeg) scrape a dusting onto the froth.
Let it soak till froth goes off.
Place poker into fire until cherry red.
Remove poker and plunge into quart.
Retrieve and replace poker.
Lift quart and drink a good half of it.
Result: Ecstasy, rapture! Repeat as required.

Cribbage, rings and dominoes were the order of the day. No
juke-boxes, no one-armed bandits, nor background music; but
the conversation was interesting and educational.

'They wor round ag'in yisday, I sin 'em!'

'Who were that, then?'

'They owd draymen, Greene King's lot, they two fat 'uns.
They downed a tidy few, but not so many as last summer,
hellabit! They druv up, the pair on 'em, settin' on that high
owd seat like a pair o' tomtits on a bull's arse. The big 'un
hollered to Bill Cooper t'fetch 'em a quart a-piece.

'They had three a-piece, lappin' their tongues round there
owd jars. The fat 'un said it worn't a bad gargle. Arter that
they got down an' come in fer a drink!'

'Ar, I well remember, come to think on it. The little 'un
wor the wust o' the pair. They reckon he put poor owd
Wimbish in his grave afore his time.'

'How wor that, then?'

'Wimbish was tidy bad, there's no denyin' . . . cancer! He
knew he wor a-gooin' but he worn't ready and towd the
drayman he wor frit to goo. He jest laughed and towd him
there worn't no need to worry about dyin', people done it
every day. There wor only one drawback, you git bloody stiff
nex' day!'

The old tales would be told and improved upon – mostly
about their working lives.

'Remember that fust harvest in Holden Field, cor blast, that
were comic! There were three on 'em. Jack an' Walt a-pitchin',
Wuddy Smith wor loadin'. Started harvest t'right. Got outside
a gallon o' dandelion wine afore breakfast. Straight arter breakfast they put paid to a gallon o' bitter. Wuddy gits in the wagon
to load. Couldn't stand, hardly. They very fust sheaf Jack

pitches to 'im 'ad a swarm o' bees in it. Wuddy got stung tidy bad, he wor too bloody drunk t'run. Talk about laugh!'

Grandfather Ford disliked the company of women and relations. One Sunday we were all invited next door to have dinner with Granny Ford – a lovely meal with lots of meat and the best vegetables. But there was no Grandad on dinner parade. He had gone to The Bonnett to dodge the cackling. Just before closing-time Granny sent my sister Poppy to The Bonnett with Grandad's dinner – in the usual basin, with top plates to keep it warm and tied down with his red and white spotted handkerchief. 'Tell 'm,' said Granny, looking more furious than I had ever seen her. 'Tell him to eat his vittels where he drinks his dratted owd beer!'

Poppy returned in five minutes – with a message. . . .

'Grandad says where's the pepper and salt?'

Opinions were expressed about the impending closure by old locals and recent locals.

'The people livin' in the hamlet today ain't the same sort as we what wukked on the land. Remember owd Quimm Walls? He allus said that if things don't alter they'll stop as they are. You mark my wuds, thing'll be alterin' tidy sharp in The Bonnett, an' fer the wuss!'

'Definitely not! We must progress. Progress is essential. The village pub has always been the most democratic institution in Britain. No social distinctions to speak of and we all know one another. We even know what everyone else is doing in the village!'

'Yew ain't far off the mark there, my owd met. You lot what's made yer money in London and come down here to buy the cottages soon find out who grows the best fruit and vegeables. You're quick on the scrounge. We ain't as daft as *you* look!'

Things did not stop as they were. The Bonnett Inn was sold. Builders, painters, decorators and furnishers swarmed round the hamlet like hornets for quite a time. And in December 1978 the cryptic scribe of *The Haverhill Echo* wrote:

BONNETT REOPENS WITH NEW LOOK AND MINUS A 'T'
Ashdon Bonnett, the pub which was auctioned off by Greene King in April for £40,000, re-opened last week after a

complete renovation. And present on the occasion to drink the first pint was Spike Mays, local author, whose book *Reuben's Corner* features the Bonnett. He has been a customer at the pub since 1914.

Mr David Norman, who bought the pub, has carried out a massive renovation scheme and is in the process of opening a restaurant upstairs in the pub.

One major change is the name of the pub, which is to be returned to the original 'Bonnet'. It was named after a Frenchman, Monsieur Bonnet, and would have been known as 'Bonnet's', but Mr Norman thinks when Greene King took it over the solicitor who draughted the documents added the extra 'T'.

Reuben's favourite fireplace had been cunningly camouflaged to make it appear older than antiquity; its chimney hook had been broken off and its root concreted in. Never again would hands stretch to reach a rose-pink ham – to cut off the succulent slices for 'levenses'; to eat them with the top of a home-made cottage loaf smarmed with farm butter the colour of marigolds, with maybe a mossel of cheese and some spring onions: a substantial meal that could be washed down with a pint of four-penny ale for an outlay of ninepence.

Now, there were chairs. Now there were stairs, to reach more chairs! Those who felt peckish had to sit at a table – to await the waiter; upstairs in the old bedroom. Instead of that brass-bound bed padded with hoss-hair mattress and pillow cases smelling of lavender, and shiny legs standing fair and square on polished oak floorboards, there were tables: ten of them, each with four chairs. Tapered and dainty their legs. Silent, non-creaky and elegant, poised rather than standing, hovering as if waiting to be bedded down on lush wall-to-wall carpetry.

Outside, where Bill Cooper kept his Gloucester Spot pigs, is a capacious car park to accommodate buses, coaches and charabancs as well as motor cars. Folk motored from all over Britain to stand in the tap-room (that was) to take a peep through its window at Brick and Stone Villa, the tied cottage we shared with our grandparents, Susannah and Reuben Ford. Many carried copies of my book, hoping I would be present

At the reopening of The Bonnet Inn

to sign them. They even scrounged copies of the posh menu card for me to sign. On that card was a copy of Grandad's portrait, painted for me by an old friend, Bill Taylor from Rochdale. The portrait was superimposed on the map I made of Ashdon and its environs to make up the endpieces. The menu artist made a good job of it, but whoever employed him forgot to ask me if I could put up with a mite of plagiarism and copyright infringement. To me it mattered not. It matters even less today. There is a reason. The Bonnet is closed. Unwanted customers arrived on the East Anglian Horizon and 'took it over'. It is now in the hands of receivers. It made me think of that old Scottish ploughman: one who drew furrows as straight as the lines of his wonderful poetry . . .

> The best laid schemes o' mice an' men
> Gang aft a-gley,
> An' lea's us nought but grief an' pain
> For promis'd joy.

Vera Basham, the lady who drew the first pint for me when The Bonnet re-opened, retired from her happy profession in June 1980. She and her husband Alec had kept The Red Lion at Steeple Bumpstead in which they lived, for the whole of their married lives. Whether or not they qualify for the *Guinness Book of Records* does not matter a lot, but I reckon they qualify for a mention in Greene King's archives for a number of excellent reasons. They did not go in for 'Pub Grub'. There was no background music. They knew how to look after Britain's best beer.

Mind you, there was plenty of music. It came from the throats of early regulars: some who had worked on the land and had retired; others who had retired from the police force, the army and the civil service. I was privileged to be one of the 'choristers'. Alec took the tenor parts. Wilf Rose, our ex-policeman, the double *fortissimo* baritone – which developed into shrill descant if he stayed until closing-time. Vera occasionally obliged with a *sotto voce* soprano, and I doubled 'twixt baritone and *basso-profundo*, toots on the tin-whistle and blasts on the 'C' Melody saxophone. Cecil Beale just made noises, mostly off-key.

Our signature tune was 'Morning has broken', but we each had our own. When Beale came in we sang his, to let Vera know who wanted what. Immediately we broke into 'There is a green hill' Vera pulled a pint of bitter. Wilf Rose's tunes varied, but we stuck to those with a rose, like 'Only a rose', 'Roses are shining in Picardy' or 'Rose Marie', any one of which meant half of Abbot. Mine was the silent version of 'All hail the power', for Alec 'There's nothing to pay' or 'Throw out the lifeline', 'Who killed Cock Robin' and 'Don't go down the mine'.

Usually we sang hymns, sometimes old ballads, and passersby would poke in their noses to spy and their ears to listen.

'They're at it ag'in. Daft as lights that lot in there. Singin' at this time o' the mornin' and couldn't hev had more'n half a pint!'

Swearing and cussin' worn't allowed. When one young lad came out with a four-letter word Alec put him in his place by handing him a piece of soap.

'Go home, lad. Off you go, and wash your mouth, it's dirty! We don't want that here!'

The Red Lion always held its own Harvest Festival, with Eric Wheeler conducting the service and leading the choir in their singing of the harvest hymns. Almost every villager turned up, laden with fruit, flowers and vegetables – first to decorate the pub and later to auction them off and raise funds for the senior citizens.

Strangers used to infiltrate and join us in song, and afterwards they aired their views . . . 'It is a most moving and heart-warming experience! We were accepted as though we belonged to the village and had lived there for years!'

'I started pulling pints of beer when I was eighteen,' said Vera. 'The only time I've been away from The Lion was for a short holiday. I remember selling mild beer at four pence a pint. Best bitter was sixpence and a nip of whisky seven pence. When I first started it was unheard of for women to come into a pub, they would sit outside and have soft drinks or half a pint. The change came during the Second World War. We were very busy and were allowed to open for only eight hours a week because beer was rationed, but there were soldiers stationed all around us and lots of Americans at Ridgewell.

Sometimes there would be a queue of a hundred or more –
waiting for opening time. Mind you, Spike, Alec and I have
pulled more than pints of beer in this old tap-room. A customer
came in with toothache one day, and Alec and I yanked the
tooth out with a pair of pliers!'

Alec told me that Vera had always aimed at creating a
friendly atmosphere and realized that living in the heart of the
country there was not a lot of passing trade so it was best to
rely on the regular customers, the village folk, and keep them
happy.

'We don't think much of the new-fangled ideas of juke-boxes
and pub grub. We have had our trade here for fifty-two years,
mostly with farmers and farm labourers, and we saw no point
in doing food as well!'

Harking back a day or two, the plain fact is that the inn is
probably the oldest institution in the English village, older
even than the church, and dates back to the Roman period,
when places of rest and refreshment were established along
newly built roads. Except in villages like Steeple Bumpstead,
the average country inn or 'pub' was little more than an
ale-house dispensing home-brewed beer to local company. But
in the heart of the country the 'pub' was the real community
centre where men who worked hard on the land gathered most
evenings for warmth and companionship.

Vera is alone now, in this village where she has played a
prominent and most friendly part. Alec died quite suddenly.
After fifty years of working together it is tragic that they could
not have a few more years together in retirement. We all miss
him, particularly the 'dawn choristers'. I probably miss him
more than most, for he taught me much and cheered me. Each
time we met we would sing just three words: 'Morning has
broken.' One day he said this . . .

'Spike, you are a happy man, and I know why. After all
these years you are back in East Anglia. You've come home,
boy. You've come home!'

15

Thatchin' an' Throshin'

On a bleak night in February I took a two-mile walk from my
bungalow to the old pub at Helions Bumpstead. In the bar of
The Three Horse Shoes sat an old school chum who used to
be a dab hand at thatching. He was not up to the standard of
Old Joslin, for Old Joslin, apart from being a cycling hot
gospeller, was a master thatcher with reed and straw. Albert
wanted to know if I had a picture of Old Joslin with his top
hat on: he always wore it after he'd finished thatching a stack
and when he was on what we used to call his 'Hallellujah
Rounds'.

I used to help my father thatch stacks. He did not thatch
the roofs of country cottages – that was a specialist's job.
Nevertheless the stack-thatching was a job which required
great patience, skill and many tools, including rakes, mallets,
knives, string and bill-hooks, plus the straw of wheat and oat
and bucket upon bucket of water. We also required 'springles'
– bunch upon bunch of them – which we used to get from
'Africa', the old nickname for Camps End, a small hamlet on
the borders of Langley Wood. Springles were wooden staples
we made from nut-hazel sticks. We rived them into four,
sharpened each end, then gave them a twist in the middle and
they were ready to staple down the thatch. We would dress for
the part in aprons made from sacks, in knee-pads made from
sturdier sacks or bits of leather, tied above and below our sore
knees with binder string. We thatched at Place Farm, then
owned by Major Tansley Luddington, and now by Edmund
Vestey.

Place Farm stacks would not be thatched too soon after
harvest. Time was required for them to heat, to let the heat
seep through before we put on the thatch. First, we would
shake up the straw with two-tined forks, then damp it

thoroughly before the process of 'yelving' – drawing out hand-fuls by using opened fingers as rakes; keeping the straw in tight straight lengths. My father would climb the ladder, beat down straggly bits of sheaves protruding from the slopes of the stack, then we would start off.

Usually he would start at the right-hand bottom corner ('That's right for my hand, boy!') putting on tidy armfuls of straightened wet straw which I carried to him up the ladder: one layer upon another, working his way up from the eaves, to the top (the ridge) where he would leave sticking up great tufts above the ridge top. These layers were secured by ham-mering in the springles I had made with my bill-hook. The process would be repeated until both sides of the stack's sloping roof were thickly thatched. But we had stacks with no sides, the round ones, plus square and rectangular ones, each requiring a separate treatment.

Last, we would put on those important touches: combing down with the rakes we had made by driving long wire nails into ashwood, followed by a short-back-and-sides trim with sheep-shears along the tufty top and the eaves; making sure they were as straight as dies for the benefit of the critics who, if the trim was a mite sorry, would broadcast the thatcher's ineptitude in the tap-rooms of every pub within reasonable drinking distance – even unto the beginning of next thatching season. Awry or not, those stacks would stand for years without one spot of rain getting through to moisten one wheat ear.

'Shame, ain't it?' said Harold. 'All they owd skills hev gone. Corse they don't need stacks no more. Ain't sin one fer years. They owd combines ruin the straw and the farmers ruin the gals' washin' by burnin' it. I reckon they owd combines are a cuss with no disguise. They ain't blessin's for sure! Tell us about owd Joslin! He's bin dead a tidy while; but I remember he a-standing on his head outside The Rose an' Crown, Ashdon, celebratin' the end of the strike just afore the Fust World War!'

In Ashdon, where he used to live along the Radwinter Road, Joslin was held to be 'a rum owd character'. Each day he would set off for thatching on his hot-gospel-bicycle, wearing his top hat, frock coat, pin-striped trousers, wing collar, cravat and spats. For bicycle-clips he wore binder string, but only in fine weather. In rain he wore over his pin-stripes his 'passion dampers': a pair of lady's bloomers.

On the near-side of his handlebars he carried his 'docky': bread and cheese, an onion and a flask of cold, milkless, unsweetened tea – tied up tramp-style in a white-spotted red kerchief. On the off-side he carried some of the tools of his two trades – some impedimenta for thatching and his hot-gospelling hand-bell.

Joslin was a religious maniac as well as a thatcher. Each time he had finished thatching a stack or a cottage he would 'Praise the Lord' by standing on his head and hands on the height of the ridge, bellowing out Baptist hymns full throttle whilst upside down. He always rode his bicycle smack in the middle of the road. One day on the Bartlow Road a motorist tried to pass him, but Joslin (who never could stand the sight of they new owd articles) would not budge until the driver gently nudged his rear wheel and deposited him, bike and all, in the ditch.

'Oh, my Brethren!' began Joslin in The Bonnett Inn . . . 'The Devil took howd on me and I had to swear. He deliberately knocked me arse-over-tip afore he asked me to put him on the right road. So I put him on two right roads – first to Cambridge, and then to Jesus!'

Joslin made the day for our villagers in Park Mede where, for the Peace Celebrations of 1919, he broke into swearing and out of his customary abstemious life. He had stayed in the beer tent and knocked back a couple of quarts of Greene King's strong ale. . . .

'I'm jest a-takin' wine ter celebrate the arse-end of this wicked owd war, my Brethren!'

Later, under the tall elms by Park Mede's entrance, he tried to sleep it off. After dimmit light, when all the birds bar owls had gone to bed and the sun had long gone down, he wakened – to see in the sky over Ashdon village a blinding white light. Scared out of his wits, bemused by his drinking, he leapt on his bicycle and pedalled furiously around the neighbouring cottages, clanking his hot-gospelling hand-bell.

'Come you on out tergither, dear brothers an' sisters!' he hollered. . . . 'This is the end of the world! Retribution hev copped us! Come you out an' be saved!'

Like most religious fanatics, Joslin had got himself steamed up unduly. The blinding glare in the night sky was not connected with the fire-and-brimstone all warmongers deserve. The village had got itself lit up deliberately with the aid of a Government surplus, ex-naval flare; so brightly indeed that folk could see to read *The Christian Herald* and the *War Cry* a good mile from the flare.

'Poddy Coote used to work alonger you at Place Farm didn't he?' said Albert. 'Well, I know he did. I see the pair on ye once. You were a-thrashin' beans in the barn. Coo, blast! That were a rum owd job. Don't you remember? Barney Bland were swingin' the sticks alonger Walt Nunn. They're all dead now. Pity, don't get men like that terday!'

'Albert, old mate,' said I. . . . 'Only yesterday I passed Ashdon Place Barn where Poddy and I used to mix all the cattle bait. I followed him from Walton's Park. He was the houseboy there before me. When I was fifteen I had to go to the farm because I was no longer a boy – so I became a man on the land without a man's pay. Six o'clock in the morning till six at night, six days a week for twelve and a tanner, but we made the best of it.'

Yes, Poddy and I used to 'swing the sticks' to get the best beans for the bean barrow, a device attached to the plough for drilling in the beans. 'The sticks' was the 'flail', a hand-threshing implement with a long wooden staff to which was attached by a leather thong a shorter, heavier stick. Poddy and I would face each other over a tarpaulin spread on the barn floor. The object of the exercise was to swing the sticks in a figure-of-eight then bring down the short stick to bash out the beans from their black pods; the earliest and most primitive method of threshing as used in biblical times. Care had to be taken in making the figure-of-eight, otherwise one would receive a hefty clout to the back of the head.

To maintain a steady rhythmical beat we used to ape the antics of church bell-ringers who used to sing jingles. Because Poddy and I were both in Ashdon church choir, we settled for hymns. One of our favourites, as we swung, swore and sweated was that good old harvest hymn 'Come, ye thankful people come', not that we had much to be thankful for during the operation. . . .

All is safely gathered in, (Thump-thump)
If it ain't it oughter bin; (Thump-thump)
All upon the barnyard floor, (Thump-thump)
For the rats and meece to gnaw. (Thump-thump)

'Hev one for the road,' said Albert. . . . 'Do you know,
Spike . . . do you know, we never had a lot, but we knew a
lot and did a lot. You take the farm labourer's job all round.
He were a highly skilled man, knew about hosses and cattle
and sheep and all they other jobs; hedgin', ditchin' – all the
year round! There worn't nothin' he couldn't do. We had
blisters on our poor owd feet and our poor owd hands. Do you
know, the only place they git blisters today is on their arses,
sittin' behind they owd tractors!' Albert knocked back his
noggin and moved to the door. 'Do you take care, Spike, owd
met. There ain't many on us left. Goodnight!'

16

There Was a Green Hill

Our first Christmas in Steeple Bumpstead was full of joy. Music, singing, conviviality, goodwill and every kind of kindness were dished out in double doses. Because Vera was bed-bound, packages, parcels, baskets and buckets were left by unknown donors. Vegetables galore, a hunk of pork dressed in a string of sausages, plus a brace of plump pheasants from Gun House. Christmas cards were 'unstamped' and were thrust through our letter-box.

Carol singers wassailed in church and chapel. Young farmers' choirs sang in village halls, the Old People's Home and in and out of places selling liquid Christmas cheer. There were parties, a pantomime and a play by the Bumpstead Players, and in the village community hall a spread was laid on for senior citizens, with a concert and knees-up.

On Christmas Eve I worked a treble shift as Father Christmas. Three school-marms of three separate schools kitted me out in scarlet robes, with hairy white beards as long as Edgware Road. My Wellies were sloshed with artificial snow. I was handed a list of pupils' names and sacks of gifts to give to the schoolchildren of two schools in Steeple Bumpstead and one in Haverhill.

'You shake hands with all the boys, and you can kiss all the girls, Mr Mays. But you must have a little drink to put you in the right mood! I had several little drinks, in and out of schools, and in the evening I was dragooned to run the Christmas raffles for The Fox and Hounds and The Red Lion.

'Bring your saxophone and give us a tune,' said Brian of The Fox and Hounds. 'You'd better have a drop of the stuff, otherwise you won't be able to play it!'

Very late that evening I created a village precedent. After prize-giving, singing carols and blasting out saxophone solos, it was brought to my attention that I had tried to play 'Away in a manger' with the mouthpiece upside down. When I rose to protest it appeared that my legs had gone on strike, and it was difficult to maintain the vertical. Outside the road was ice-encrusted. PC Marks came to my aid and kindly escorted me down the darkness and ice. Kenneth was in uniform. Beams of headlights floodlit us: voices came through the night. . . .

'What the hell's gooin' on, then?'

'What's the hold-up?'

'Have you arrested Father Christmas, Ken?'

'He is under arrest on two charges, mate . . . playing carols upside down, and for gettin' his beard tangled up with keys of a musical instrument. Goodnight! Happy Christmas to you!'

Our first Christmas in Steeple Bumpstead took me back to Christmas in Ashdon, when I was eleven. I will always remember its sadness. One month earlier most of our folk in little Bartlow Hamlet had given thanks in Ashdon's church of All Saints. For four years, mammoth casualty lists had appeared in *The Saffron Walden Weekly News*. But on the eleventh hour of the eleventh month of 1918 joy percolated our hitherto joyless land. That senseless slaughter of the more senseless fighting in Flanders had finished. In prayer and song we gave our thanksgiving – in the church before we celebrated the signing of the Armistice with fêtes, frolics and fireworks in Park Mede. Those of our menfolk who had been spared went back to their productive work on the fertile fields: long-neglected fields. In the evenings we boys and girls were out and about ganging up for the carol singing.

We made our own lanterns, old jam-jars with string handles in which we waxed in stumps of candles. We wore muffs, funny leggings fashioned from old oat sacks to keep snow from skinny legs; and in our canvas muffs we toted hand-warmers. Our villagers could see us for miles, for our straggling, candle-torched procession was easily discerned in our otherwise light-less land. We felt happy and Christmassy as we stood on farmers' and cottagers' doorsteps: all red of cheek, with our frost-misted breath spurting in pale pinks and mellow yellows, floodlit by soft candlelight.

When we sang at Whiten's Mere Farm I remembered that my favourite uncle Bert Whistler had been killed by German machine-gun bullets, only a few months after he had been commissioned in the South Staffordshire Regiment. Cousin Dorothy, his daughter, was singing with us. Others had lost fathers, but ours had been spared to us after five woundings, one with mustard gas. I thought how marvellous it would be for cousin Dorothy and the others if their fathers could be lifted from the mud of Flanders to sing with us, just for Christmas.

Those of us whose fathers had returned from that mysterious place all the newspapers called 'The Front' hung up our stockings for nuts, sweets, apples and (maybe) an orange. Oranges were thin on village grounds because the Germans' 'U-boats' had cancelled deliveries. Those without fathers didn't bother, they knew who the real Santa Claus was (or had been), and that mothers could not fill stockings without one.

All Saints' was packed for the Christmas. Though some women cried this singing was better than Easter or Harvest Thanksgiving . . .

> God from on high hath heard
> Let sighs and sorrow cease.
> Lo! from the opening heav'ns descends
> To man the promised peace.

Out in the snow the women gathered in little groups, some all in black and with their faces veiled. Others were dabbing at their eyes with handkerchiefs, making false laughter to cheer up others – and telling horrible lies. . . .

'Things'll be all right from now on!'

'There won't be no more wars, thank God!'

Fifty-seven years later, after attending the Remembrance Service with the local branch of the Royal British Legion, at Steeple Bumpstead, I sat at a table in the bar of The Red Lion with 'Porky' (Bert Eppy). He had been on parade with us and cried when we stood to attention for the silence. Our memorial stone is deeply etched with villagers' names who had served with him in the First World War in The Suffolks, the 'Dutty Dozen', 12th of Foot.

'I couldn't march, Spike, on account o' me poor owd feet. How did the Service go?'

I told him that in his address the Vicar had reminded us that plans were afoot to cancel Remembrance Day. It didn't sink in at first, he spoke about the name-reading . . . 'Bunny done that well.'

Ex-Squadron Leader 'Bunny' Rymills, DFC, DFM, had read out the names of the village dead in two world wars. The same family names in each, one generation after another. He read them most reverently and clearly. We could feel the grief. It took longer to read those names than we had to stand for the silence.

Porky thumped his mug on the table, he looked whully riled for the penny had dropped.

'Cancel it! They marn't do that . . . Hellabit! Whatever would my owd mets say if they could come back? What would they say?' He gave me a nudge. . . . 'You know where I were when the fust Armistice got signed? I'll tell yer. I were in Beirut where some daft buggers hev just started fightin' ag'in!'

Ex-Private Bertram Eppy was one of our then two survivors of the First World War. He was very bad on his pins through contracting trench foot and his little legs almost rotted away. But he was a jolly countryman whose eyes were bright as new horse chestnuts and twinkled when we sang the old songs he loved: 'There's a long, long trail a-winding' and 'Mademoiselle from Armentiers'.

Porky has ended his long, long trail – or should it be 'trial'? But we managed to take a snifter together before he died. He looked so sad.

'What's up, Porky, mate? Have you signed the Pledge?'

'Hellabit, Spike! I've bin thinkin'.'

'About what?'

'That there film on TV last night. They called it *The Green Hill Pals* and I hope they daft buggers watched it.'

'What daft buggers?'

'Them wicked sods who wanter cancel Remembrance Day!'

Everybody knows the hymn 'There is a green hill far away', but not everybody knows of a green hill about ten miles from Steeple Bumpstead. It is a public house and is owned by Greene King and stands in Linton, Cambridgeshire. The story goes that a former landlord of the establishment would not sell a gill of beer to a potential customer unless he sang the opening line; but a stop was put to the custom when the Americans 'came over here'. Some knew the words, but none could sing.

I was in The Green Hill on a day in January. From its tap-room window can be seen the tower of Linton Church. I was also in the church on that day, for it was there that we said farewell to Laurie Fuller.

Normally quiet and peaceful, Linton wasn't a mite peaceful on that day. There were almost as many motors there as clutter Piccadilly; and as many coppers as they turn out there to keep a sharp lookout on its hippies and junkies. Our policemen friends were not there to keep order – there was no need. They had turned out a hundred-strong to line the path to Linton Church – to pay last respects to one of their former members.

After Laurie had served his time and won his campaign medals in the Grenadier Guards he became, among other things, a village policeman in Linton. When he retired from the police he had made plans to continue his active life as a blacksmith, for Laurie was an artist in ironwork. He was chairman of the Histon Branch of the Grenadiers' Association. He sometimes wore the kilt of the 'Gallant Forty-twa' (The Black Watch, 42nd of Foot) and he played the bagpipes.

In his capacity as village policeman he was venerated. And then he died. . . .

We will miss him, and have missed him, but will remember him. How moving, yet cheering, to see the immaculate turnout of the police! In their dark-blue, with silvery buttons, boots and shoes shining like mirrors. Some wore campaign medals and police medals. Some had served with Laurie in the Grenadier Guards. Dark-blue and silver were paying tribute to scarlet and gold. Not a word of command was uttered, or whispered. Old habits and training die hard. Almost immediately a Guard of Honour was formed by Old Comrades, who formed up and lined the road to the church. As the Bible-black Daimler bore Laurie past the ranks, one saw a ram-rod stiffening of backs. Heels clicked. Old soldiers and young policemen stood like statues; thumbs behind the seams of trousers, and heads held high.

There came a pregnant hush as the casket was shoulder-hoisted. Richly flower-bedecked it bore colours of Police and the Household Division. Upon that cushion glistered Laurie's

Brother Leslie

campaign medals for active service in the Grenadiers and dedicated service in the Cambridgeshire Constabulary. Manly chins wobbled and eyes misted, including mine as I thought of that old adage . . . 'Old soldiers never die, they only fade away.' Words flashed to mind. Words taught to me in Ashdon Elementary School before I 'went for a soldier'. . . .

> Not a drum was heard, not a funeral note,
>   As his corse to the rampart we hurried;
> Not a soldier discharged his farewell shot
>   O'er the grave where our hero we buried.

The words were not strictly true. Laurie was not buried. There were no muffled drums. Not a shot was fired. There were, however, funeral notes – from an ex-Grenadier Drummer who had brought his bugle. Out of practice, he cracked only one note. Later, with a tear in his eye, he spoke to my brother who had been a Grenadier Drummer sixty years earlier, after his release from the harsh treatment of a prisoner-of-war camp for four miserable years. . . .

'I buggered it up, Les, mate. One bad note! It's dead easy sounding Last Post as a routine call, but bloody tough sounding it for somebody you know, like Laurie.'

Service over, we motored through Cambridge towards Huntingdon, a cortège convoy to the crematorium. Half of us could not get into the little chapel. Parson's murmurings could be heard, then clear notes shrilled. Heels clicked, our shoulders squared and our chins were drawn in. Les Ager's notes rang out from a silver cornet. (Ager was once in the band of the Norfolk's; he is now the Musical Director of the Haverhill Silver Band.) When he played the last two notes, one low and the last high which lifts the call to E, the anthem was over. As always, it carried the minds of us ex-soldiers from the limit of the known – the end of a day, or a soldier's life – to the infinity of unknown tomorrow.

'Let's go and see the flowers,' said brother Leslie.

Like Grenadiers at Horse Guards for Colour Trooping the flowers were in immaculate 'dress'; rank upon rank, including seventy-two wreaths. Some beribboned in silver and blue; others in scarlet and blue. Some were all blood-red, the scarlet poppies of branches of the Royal British Legion. There were many more from relations and friends. All had cards expressing comradeship and love.

Les and I motored back to Helions Bumpstead, the village where we were schoolboys when the Germans were killing the fathers of our fellow schoolboys and had wounded our father five times. We charged our glasses. We drank to an absent friend. Brother Les was deeply moved. Night after night he had sat with Laurie and was with him when he died. Silenced by cruel cancer of the throat; that voice so full of humour and kindness.

'What would old Laurie reckon to his send-off, Grenadier Mays?'

'You should know. You came to our meeting at Histon British Legion when he was in the chair. I reckon he'd say something like this . . . 'Gentlemen of the Guards, and men of other regiments. We have completed every item of our agenda. I declare this meeting closed. Fall out for drinks!'

We had the 'other half', to Laurie. A last verse crashed into my mind. . . .

> Slowly and sadly, we laid him down,
>   From the field of his fame fresh and gory;
> We carved not a line, and we raised not a stone,
>   But we left him alone with his glory.

17

Wine and Women – and One Song

I paid an inquisitive visit to Camps End, a spreading hamlet adjoining Castle Camps, Shudy Camps and lovely Langley Wood. Long ago Camps End had been nicknamed Little Africa. No one knows why. A wine you may never have tasted used to be made there by a farm-hand who claimed it had the power of palliatives, the punch of purgatives and the balm of balsam. It would silence whooping cough, bring out 'tidy quick' the rashes of measles and chicken-pox, take the sting out of nettle-rash and put in-growing toenails in reverse. Above all it was East Anglia's finest aphrodisiac. . . .

'Tha's whully powerful, my owd met. That make weak men strong an' strong men impossible. You ask the gels!'

Pipper Free has been dead a long time. Comfrey still grows in Langley Wood – the wine is a product from its roots. If you happen to spot a tall ditch plant with very rough leaves bearing clusters of bell-like white and purple flowers, you've hit the Jackpot. You're on to Comfrey. You can make wine. Here is the recipe . . .

Comfrey wine

Dig out roots, peel and slice into strips.
(Wear gas-mask. It stinks!)
Put in cauldron and add water, a gallon to each four roots.
Boil with lid off until roots are soft.
Strain liquid through muslin and throw away roots.
Add to liquid three pounds preserving sugar.
Simmer one hour.
Pour liquid into earthenware jug.
Cover with cloth.
Stir daily for ten days.
When finished working (fermenting) pour into cask or jars.

Leave for three months.
Throw away pulp, warn neighbours where.
Add sugar and lemon juice.
Strain and bottle, leaving corks free.
As fermentation continues top up bottles (surplus liquid).
When wine is at rest tighten corks.
Leave for three months.

Other country wines can be made without the prospect of developing uncontrollable sexual drives, and cheaply. Few utensils were needed for Granny Ford's bakehouse distillery: barrels from the publican at sixpence a-piece sawn in half to make two mashers; a few stone jars ranging from half-gallon to four-gallon, and some wooden casks. After a clean-up with spring water Granny would immerse flowers, fruit and roots in more clear spring water for several weeks. From time to time she would skim away the surface scum. When ready, the juice would be strained through fine muslin into the jars and demerara sugar added. The juice was put into her iron boiler and heated, stirred and left to ferment. Brewer's yeast was used to aid fermentation, either by dissolving it in the liquid, or by placing yeast on a slice of bread and letting it float on the surface for a day or two. After standing for the prescribed period, according to the variety of fruit, the wine was poured into broaching casks, and corked loosely to allow it to 'breathe'. Once it had fermented, corks and bungs were driven home. According to the contents the casks, bottles and jars were labelled and carefully dated in Sunday-best handwriting. Because she lacked a calendar Granny caused consternation. Just below COW-SLIP she printed THIS YEARS.

Many wines were made from nature's larders, the allotments, gardens, fields and meadows: parsnip, rhubarb, wheat, dandelion, barley, sorrel and cowslip. Although elderberries are profuse and easily gathered they were not much used for wine in the 1920s. In the war of 1914–1918 our bread was spread with elderberry jam, and we were glad of it. Grandfather Ford liked best of all Granny's hip wine. Made from the shiny scarlet pods of the wild rose, it was nectar: a delicate liqueur. Grandad would sip and sniff, roll his tongue round his chops, then give instructions. . . .

'Thasser tidy drop, Sue. But marn't be meddled oo fer a
year or more. Ain't best till it's seen a spring or two. Knock
the bung in, *now*!'

Joslin the hot-gospelling thatcher worn't all that partial to
Granny's hip wine. . . .

'Very nice, Susan!' Then, in whispers to Grandad. . . .
'Don't seem to tickle the owd gizzard like Sue's parsnip. Praise
the Lord!'

An old friend of mine who once lived in Little Wratting,
Suffolk, moved down to the Garden of England, not all that
far from Canterbury. He believed that all good things from
Mother Earth should be used, not wasted by protection. He
got himself into hot water, poor chap, for making more use
than most of windfall apples – and this without being any
kind of authorized person at all! On patrolling his estate one
September day he reached the conclusion that his apple trees
were not producing all they might. Not being over-partial to
solid food his mind flashed to 'cider'. At the time he was
knee-high in windfalls.

Presently, he set to work on rounding up his fallen fruit.
With friends, he mobilized in his cellar every basin, pot, jug,
tub and barrel in and out of reach. Old trouser presses were
pressed into cider action. Innumerable apples were pulped,
pressed, squeezed and squashed. Juice dripped from basin to
pot, from pot to pan and jug to tub, until two hefty barrels
brimmed with the life-giving liquid. For two months the cider
was left to its own devices, and might well have been forgotten
for all time had not the beady eye of my thirsty friend lit upon
a book about cider manufacture. It recommended the addition
of alcohol to all maturing cider to assist the manifold processes
of fermentation. Gin, in particular, was a desirable additive.

This seemed to make such good sense that he took two
bottles of gin and poured one into each barrel. Next morning
he repeated the dose, thinking he might have erred on the
niggardly side. He left the book lying about the house. His
wife read it. As a kindly surprise to her husband, she added a
bottle apiece to each barrel. Quietly the cider went on its
way, doing its daily dozen like Eileen Fowler and going from
strength to strength.

One day when the parson was present – with a throat as dry

Granny and Grandad Reuben Ford

as a bishop's – it was decided that the cider should be tapped. The butler disappeared into the depths of the cellar. Presently, there was a strong smell of apples and juniper, following the appearance of the butler, bearing a silver tray with seven silver pots of the cider.

'We drank our delicious cider,' said my friend, and continued. . . .

'Personally, I can remember nothing more of what happened on that day. Nor, on comparing notes later, did I find a shred of memorizing among the others. But the Parson, God bless him! passed out.'

Memories would not have been obliterated and the parson would have remained erect if, instead of cider, my friend had served them Comfrey. Alas, alas! it is no longer made in this neck of the woods. The ancient distilleries no longer exist because the old 'Backhouse' has been banished. There are no keelers, nary a peeler, and no tell-tale. If Granny Ford knew this she would rise in wrath from her Bartlow resting place, roll up her sleeves and build a new one. And this is the reason . . .

Grandfather Reuben Ford was one who used to work in the Backhouse from time to time to help Granny Ford – when he was not too busy being horse-keeper at Overhall Farm for nigh on sixty years. He always tethered his plough team to five-barred gates (if there was one near the field) when he ate his docky (elevenses). He would eat a bit of a cottage loaf made by Granny Ford, in the Backhouse. Sometimes he'd take a sliver of raw onion with it, and a mite of cheese. Before resuming his ploughing he would wash down his docky with home-brewed beer, made by himself, in the Backhouse.

The Backhouse, and every tied cottage had one, was the class-room, college, university and factory. Every cottage housewife was taught by her mother the arts of mixing, firing, kneading and watching, to make loaves and bakestones in the brick ovens of the Backhouse. Most fathers taught their boys to brew.

My heart fell when I went back to Brick and Stone Villa. The 'factory' had vanished. I remembered Granny Ford and her fortnightly ritual of baking. She prepared the dough overnight, placing careful measures of wheat flour in her kneading trough, the keeler. Her 'secret measures' of salt and water were added and a little mysterious 'something' to the yeast, a family secret. When it was thoroughly mixed, the wooden lid of the keeler was pressed hard down on the dough and covered with warmed sacks to assist fermentation. By morning the lid would have been forced off, and Granny would press down gently with the back of her hands all over the sacking to expel the gas. Then she would become far less gentle as she did her dough-bashing, shaping and moulding on the upturned lid of the keeler, to bash out a big lump for the base and a small one for the top. A cottage loaf had been created!

Reuben's task was to bring the oven to baking heat for 'temperature' was of paramount importance. Deep inside the clay-plastered oven he placed an ignited faggot of blackthorn. With cunningly directed jets of air from his 'bellerses' (bellows) he would puff the fire to white heat. Then he would take a peep at the 'watch and tell-tale', a small pebble specially selected from some field, which changed colour with variations of temperature. The 'tell-tale' was built into the wall of the oven. When it became fiery red he would rake the faggot embers into the recess below the oven, which was then cleaned with a mop made of sacking tied to a pole and saturated with spring water.

When all was free from rust, dust and burnish Granny would burst into the act again. Like a Bengal Lancer she would hold the 'peel' – a long circular spoon of board mounted on a wooden handle – and one by one each loaf was placed, or spooned, into the oven and left to bake. She then scrubbed down her precious keeler – a much prized gift on her wedding-day from the village wheelwright – and would stand sniffing away at the wonderful smell of the baking bread. Quick sniffs indicated the bread was nearly done, for it was by smell she knew when it was properly baked. She would 'cop howd' of her steel-bladed peeler, slide it under the loaves and draw them out carefully and leave them to cool. Her fortnightly baking was done, and we children would be called, and given a sample: the hot top of a cottage loaf – smelling and tasting so deliciously of wheat and heat-softened cheese.

Not a mite of the oven's heat was allowed to be wasted, for

the hand-cut faggots had to be carried on backs from woods and hedgerows; and they cost a tanner a-piece to buy. King Teddy spuds were placed in the glowing embers. Never since have baked potatoes tasted so good. Pots, pans and galvanized pails filled with hot water from the still hot copper over the oven were poured into the zinc bath. Baking day was bath day. The whole family, often two at a time and regardless of sex discrimination, washed away a fortnight's dirt.

Twice a year the copper was used for an event of equal consequence, for it was ale day. Licking his lips, surrounded by odd-sized sacks of berries, hops, malt and yeast, Grandad Reuben wished not to be disturbed by man or beast, even when he watched and waited for the twenty-four gallons of good spring water to creep to the boil. He poured it over the malt in the keeler, gave frenetic and furious stirrings, then added sugar and hops. When cool it was sampled by adults and children alike, at the stage of the 'sweet wat', but we were not encouraged to drink much of it for it was intended for the hard toiler in the fields and, if good enough, for entry and judgement in fêtes and flower shows. Brought back to the boil, the yeast was added and the brew was left to settle for five hours. It had become strong brown ale, and was strained into casks, enough to last through seed time to harvest.

Other than the zinc and copper containers, every article used in home-brewing was home-made; keelers, stirring paddles, ladles, casks and taps. Fewer utensils were needed for Granny Ford's wine-making: a few stone jars ranging from half a gallon to four gallons, and some wooden casks.

'There's no doubt about it, owd Susan could sartinly make a tidy drop when she got down to it,' said Walt Stalley, who lived next door. 'I reckon the best she makes is cowslip, but Reuben fancies piss-bed dandelion. Dandelion you hev to wait for. That marn't be touched or meddled oo for a year or more. Don't seem ter tickle the owd gizzard like the cowslip!'

Granny had a little book she passed on to my mother. I have it now, all creased and yellow with age and fruit-stained and I passed on the recipes to friends in Steeple Bumpstead. . . .

Cowslip

Gather two pecks of cowslips.
Lay to dry in sun for few days.
Take eighteen quarts of water.
To each gallon add three pounds of raw sugar – put on fire.
When nearly boiling put in well-beaten whites of two eggs.
Boil one hour.
Allow to cool.
When lukewarm put in cowslips, juice and peel of three lemons
   and two tablespoons yeast.
Stir well twice a day for three or four days.
When fermentation stops strain through sieve into barrel.
Bung tight.
Stand for nearly one month.
NB: If bottling, add one lump sugar to each bottle.

Women in the hamlet were dab-hands at making other wines: parsnip, rhubarb, wheat, barley, beet, potato and carrot. In 1920 they all turned their attention to making wine from the elderberry. 'That's wholly good fer colds. Makes you sweat it out!'

Walt Stalley told us about the East Anglian cold cure.

'You know an ordinary house brick's gotter frog: that holler bit the brick-layers put most o' the mortar in. . . . Well, when you go to bed a-nights you take a brick and half-fill the frog with water. Set it down on the floor, the side where you sleep. Then, when your cold goes down to drink you bugger orf an' leave it!'

In the bar of Steeple Bumpstead's Red Lion, I discussed the old wine and beer-making with Bertie Willett. All his life a farm-worker and horse-keeper he is three months my senior in age, and my mentor in the delightful game of bowls.

'Have you ever made beer or wine, Bertie, boy?'

'I've helped, but I've put down more'n I ever made; could do with a pint of home-brewed right now, this stuff ain't much cop. No taste, all gas and now they've put it up ag'in you can't git two pints onnit fer a quid. Dunno what things are a-comin' to. That pub in Bury St Edmunds called The Nutshell. They

reckon it's the smallest pub in England. The price ain't small,
tho'. They reckon it's the cost of transport what puts the price
up. That's a packer lies. Greene King Brewery is jest opposite,
acrorst the road. Makes y'think, don't it?'

'How about wine?'

'Only bought beer. Y'know, Spike, I drank beer afore I
went to wuk. The men could get a pint o' the best and five
Woodbines for only a tanner. It's over a quid now f' twenty
Players. Coo! Makes y'think!'

'How about home-made wine?'

'Some onnit's all right. As long as the old uns make it.
Young uns don't know how an' don't wanna know, but it ain't
all their fault.'

'Whose fault is it?'

'Farmers. Never satisfied. Allus on the grab! They reckon
if farmers were ghosts they wouldn't give anybody a fright.
They worn't allus like it, but they git wuss an' wuss. Some on
it's due t'tractors an' combine harvesters. Had t'cut the hedges
down. Don't plough headlands no more, like we did with
hosses. When the hedges goo all the wild fruit goos: black-
berries, nuts, sloes an' crab apples. We boys used t'git a tanner
a peck. They used to make sloe wine, crab-apple jelly, whully
beautiful. They git it in tins today. Gals don't do no walkin'
like they used to. Even take the child'en to school in motors,
less than quarter of a mile!'

'Have a pint alonger me.'

'Not now. See yer ternight on the bowlin' green. We're
havin' a rollup. Bring yer woods. Cheerio! Do you take care,
there ain't many on us left!'

Bertie, whom everybody calls 'Butty' was a bachelor, who
lived with bachelor brothers at Waltons, a smallholding about
three miles out of our village. He never mentioned women,
loathed smutty stories, but joined full throttle in our sing-
songs, especially in our roundelay 'Who killed Cock Robin'.
We got on well. Bertie made me think!

We had both started off working on the land. Bertie never
left it. Within a month or two we were of the same age, but
we had led quite different lives. I tried to fathom why we were
so alike, and yet so different. Most men and mawthers who,
like Bertie and me, are the wrong side of the allotted span of

three score years and ten, have developed a few idiosyncrasies and individual traits – more personally and gratifyingly welcomed as convictions and beliefs. But we are forever changing. No matter how we try to avert it, that soft clay of our early impressionable years gets pounded into different shapes. Our nice, innocent mawkish softness goes off, sets like cement. So quickly that, before we can holler 'Boo' to a gander, we begin grating and jarring on others who have not had our experiences in life, or do not hold our points of view. This is certainly true about three topics not supposed to be yapped about in saloon bars, but remaining the chief points of conversation: religion, politics, sex! Usually in reverse order.

From time to time, usually when I meet Bertie at bowls or in a bar, I find it delightful to remember the soft clay of peasants: perhaps the softest of all clays, forever being ranted about by poets, but seldom by peasants. I found equal delight when the late Sir John Betjeman in a talk reminded us so kindly of our first loves, of that lovelorn lunacy, and the beauty of it all before sex took over and re-shaped that old, old pattern, when life and love were new.

For almost a year – until August 1921, when I had to leave my elementary school at Ashdon – I had fluctuated 'twixt peaks of exhilaration and troughs of despair. I was as blithesome as a bird, when *she* smiled; damp and dismal as ditch-water, when *she* seemed not to notice me. We hardly spoke. We were both so shy. Somehow we knew we had something to share, sometime.

When first our eyes met to play havoc with my mind I had become acutely aware of inferiority. I felt I needed gayer plumes. A new suit would do the trick, instead of grandfather's old cut-downs. A rejuvenation of my outward appearance, a reinvigoration of my wit, the aptitude swiftly and accurately to answer my schoolmaster's trickiest questions when he orally tested our class in the 'big room' might also help. Whether or not I knew the answer my hand had to be the first one raised. I prayed that other boys' answers should be wrong. That my teacher come to me for the right answer. Just to please *her*! She was never out of my mind. Because of her I lived in a realm of constant day-dreaming, hallucination and fantasy. I was *her* hero, *her* professor, *her* Sir Galahad and Saint George.

Every one of those questions was a dragon, ogre or wicked knight to be slain with the sharp sword of my wit, for my Ladye.

I was in love. *She* knew. Her face betrayed her. I did not dare tell her. For months we were equally evasive and elusive, and led each other a pretty dance – until that letter came. She had left our little village for distant London, but she wrote. . . . 'Back to Ashdon next week. See you in school. Love, Nellie.'

I tore to my tiny bedroom to read my first love letter – a thousand times.

I could and should have spoken to her when we broke class, but she was with other girls and I was shy. I skulked along the allotment path, screened from the road by dense hawthorn. She looked back, loitered, then halted smack in the road by the hedge gap. I stepped through the gap and stood like an oaf.

She came to me.

So close that the light wind tickled her hair into my face, like an angel's kiss. For a moment we stood face to face, but inches apart; and looked at each other not saying a word.

Later, we walked together endless measures of foot-pathed fields, hipped and hawed hedgerows and emerald meadows; clutching their old beauty to our new young hearts. Butterfly kisses would be exchanged, like withered leaves and thistledown meeting in the wind.

There are not poet's poems, nor is there maestro's music, to tell how our hearts sang when we were young and so in love. . . .

But old East Anglians write to me, thanking that I have reminded them of their love and softness. Sometimes they come to see me, in Lily Corner, Water Lane.

Perhaps the poet Robert Southey in his 'The Curse of Kegana' written way back in 1810 summed it up for us:

> They sin who tell us Love can die,
> With life all other passions fly,
> All others are but vanity.
> In heaven Ambition cannot dwell.

Nor Avarice in the vaults of hell;
Earthly these passions of the earth,
They perish where they had their birth.

But Love is indestructible;
Its holy flame for ever burneth,
From heaven it came, to heaven returneth.

Too oft on earth a troubled guest,
At times deceived, at times oppressed.
It here is tried and purified.
Then hath in heaven its perfect rest;
It soweth here with toil and care,
But the harvest-time of Love is there.

Sixty years have gone by since that grudging tearful farewell, but the harvest-time is not over. Under the high skies of spring and hot summer when flowers erupt and green turns to gold, even in blustery March and weeping April, she is with me, in the kiss of the winds and the scent of Suffolk's bean-flowering, and the blossoming of scraggy, spiky thistles into blue Gardenias.

On the day I returned to Anglia a letter came from a married couple in Ugley, Essex. The lass was then seventy-seven, her lad a mere stripling of seventy-four. He had been a farmhand all his life; they have never left their village. I shall cherish their words. . . . 'We know all the villages you have written about and we well remember the hardship of those early years. But we are still together and are very happy. A thing people don't seem to know much about these days — according to the papers. Give me the good old days, and thank you for enabling us to relive them.' They two'll do for my sex symbol.

18

Sing a Song o' Chitterlings

Jovial Ted Sissons, a well-loved 'character' and a roadman employed by Haverhill District Council, has a wonderful wife so generous of heart and mind that she considers a day to be wasted if she has failed to do someone a good turn. Ted calls her 'My owd wukkin' gal'. A first-class cook of good plain food, she specializes and excels at making brawn (in Suffolk 'pork cheese') and is also a dab-hand at preparing a local delicacy from pig's bellies, much loved by Suffolk villagers and named 'chitterlings'. I am extremely partial to both. So much so that Les Humphries – the ex-cattle king – contrives to nourish me with either or both. Les has a brother who used to live in Steeple Bumpstead and who recently moved to Ashdon. Before a vegetarian could say 'spare ribs' he had re-opened Ashdon's closed butcher's shop, and he now purveys both of those dishes, and sends some to me. In the course of one short morning I received pork cheese from Ted and chitterlings from Les. My day was made. I still salivate at the merest recollection. Chitterlings are now gaining recognition and may be purchased at quite a number of butchers in East Anglia. They were more popular when most homesteads kept a pig, and pork was the staple meat diet.

My good friend Christopher wrote the story about Mike and his wife 'Polly Mike' – we both knew them when they lived in a tiny cottage down Church Hill, Ashdon. His real name was Mike Wilson. He kept pigs, to eat. He knew little of anything else. Slow of speech and wit, he was also round-shouldered, for which he blamed the low ceiling of his cottage. His wonderful wife was affectionately known as 'Polly Mike' because they were so inseparable. After a partnership of fifty years Polly anticipated his every whim. In his undemonstrative way he worshipped her 'Owd Owly', on account of her large round spectacles. 'She do look like a grut owl oo they there glasses on' was really an endearing term, making Polly smile, and sometimes blush.

Unlike the farmers' pigs, Mike's did not get a diet of skimmed milk, boiled and mashed pig-taters, nor meal, mash and root crops. Just the scraps, but Polly allus paid for the pollard (or bran) to mix with the swill.

Business was her responsibility. Mike did the work: fed and mucked out the pigs and stacked their steaming manure – to fill Church Hill with its ripe odour. When killing time neared Mike would see Sonny Pearson, village butcher and slaughterer. Mike would know when, by the ever-increasing proportions of his Middle White or Gloucester Spot as they fed at the trough, and checked by keeping a crafty lookout on the moon. He kept to the country norms . . .

> Allus kill a pig when the moon's a-waxin'
> Never killun when she be wastin';
> Do, an' the pork'll be fit fer nuthin'
> An' the fat'll wast oo the moon.

A short walk would confirm that Sonny was willing to kill. Mike would get out his mash tubs. Polly would prepare the earthenware pan for the curing, and put ready sugar, salt, beer and saltpetre. Some pigs were killed at the butcher's, but Mike always had his killed in his backyard . . . 'to kitch all the blood ter make black puddens'. The pigs allus shrieked and hollered, but the death was painless. Mike added his strength to Sonny's to swing the pig into boiling water. He would scrape the hair from its hide with comb-like knives, draw it, open it from throat to tail, and insert an ash stick across the belly-cut to keep the carcase open. They would then hang the pig from a branch of Mike's stunted and fruitless apple tree. . . .

'I allus hang the bugger there, 'cos there ain't a mossel o' room inside. That owd ceilin' ain't high enough!'

Next day Sonny would return to dress and cut the carcase, set the different cuts aside for Polly to wrap in pieces of linen and muslin, and cart away all the pork left over.

Mike and Polly lived right royally on the liver of the pluck, and in those days one could buy a whole pig's pluck for a tanner, curtains and all: those bits of laced fat in which they fried onions and liver.

The worst job was the cleaning of the 'chitluns', as most of us called them. They were washed in hot and cold water several times, and during this process Mike would sniff and say . . . 'Damn an' blast, thasser tidy owd pong! That cut off the light o' the sun!'

Polly prepared the chitterlings as gifts for her neighbours, and did the job to rights. She would soak them in salt water, and turn them each day until they blushed a rosy pink, ready for the pot. After boiling and straining them she would do what she called her 'secret trick': put them out in the sunshine, on the grass under the stunted apple tree – where they could be seen by all! When dried off they were gleaned from the grass, packed or wrapped in muslin ready for the children to collect and take to their homes. All waxy white, rich and clean – and 'more-ish'.

Sometimes we ate them cold with a simple sauce of vinegar and mustard like the farm labourers did in the pub; but *we* could not wash them down with a pint of good ale. And when we had the Chitterling Suppers in the village hall which Anglia's folk relished, sometimes salivating in anticipation, they were served hot with hunks of bread, usually the tops of home-made cottage loaves, smarmed with a dollop of rich farm butter the colour of marigolds. They had been fried to a golden brown and were served with a rasher of bacon and a slice or two of pig's liver. For 'Finishers' there were hunks of caraway seed cake and ginger cake, washed down with home-made wine: elderberry, dandelion, and 'rubbub'.

And then we used to sing because our hearts and bellies were filled – with joy and pig's guts! As they used to say, my belly-button's a long way from my owd backbone!

However, on pig-killing night at Church Hill all was solemn and a mite eerie. As darkness fell the ghostly shape of the carcase seemed to be floating in mid-air, not suspended from the tree. Mike could not be seen by anybody. . . .

Snuggled in his thick, black overcoat, squatting on the seat of his outdoor privy with his eyes fully peeled, Mike could see everything. Loaded with no. 4 shot, with hammer at full cock and percussion cap in firing position, his ancient single-barrelled lay cradled across his knobbly knees. Mike was on pig-guard, ready for instant action. He would watch the oil lamp go out as Polly puffed down its glass. She was about to climb 'wooden hill', to bed down all alone; the only times in sixty years they were ever separated.

Chitterlings are coming back for human consumption, thank heavens! But if Les and Ted had not brought their gifts, old Mike and his porker might well have remained in the vault of lost memory. So, some sixty years after Mike's sentinel squatting in Ashdon, I had chitterlings for breakfast and song for supper.

19

Time, Gentlemen, Please

Years ago, on Hungerton Field I was dung-spreading with PC
Kenneth Marks's uncle, Wuddy Smith. We could not afford
watches like that old gamekeeper of Waltons! 'That were
advertised in *The Saffron Walden Weekly News*. A real Hinger-
sole, with phosphor paint on the black dial for night-looking.
Yew could see the daylight time in the bluddy dark. I sent
forrit. Proper bargain, on'y twelve bob!'

Wuddy was watchless. Like me he told the time by watching
the shadows made by trees and hedgerows, the time when
birds flew high or low, and when rabbits and hares popped in
or out.

On that dung-spreading morning a new motor-car pulled
up. We had only two motors in our village, so this was new to
us.

'He's wavin' his arm, boy,' said Wuddy. . . . 'Goo an' see
what he want. No! Howd yew hard. I'll goo. Might be a man's
job!'

I went to the headland with Wuddy who asked, 'Wotcher
want, then?'

'The time. I'm late, can you tell me the time?'

Wuddy looked at shadows, sky, clouds, birds and finally
cast an eye along the piles of steaming dung. He cleared his
throat and rasped out a mite of assistance. . . . 'By the time
we've spread a couple more heaps, I reckon it'll be abowt a
quarter arter 'leven.'

'That's not much help,' said the timeless one.

'More ain't yew, metty. . . . Bugger orf!'

Much time has been misspent by many people over countless
ages, of divers races, colours, creeds and customs, of complex
virtues, vices and vocations; all having a bash at defining
'Time'. My old dung-spreading partner would sum up their

Alec and Vera of The Red Lion

attempts pretty sharp. . . . 'A bloody waste o' time!' Would
Wuddy be far off the mark? He would be handicapped. He
could not read. He could count a bit, just his wages. It didn't
take long: just ten and a tanner a week.

To think that I had to wait sixty years, until my return to
Anglia, to learn the truth about that patched prisoner-of-war:
a German soldier who worked on the farmers' fields by day and
slept each night with the wife of an English soldier defending us
in Flanders. Rough music had been played to alert the villagers;
traps were set to catch him; but he escaped the villagers' 'rough
justice', even with a gammy leg. . . .

'Father said, they nearly had him once. They were chasin'
the bugger across Woodshot field, jest bin ploughed. He had
one leg a good three inches shorter than t'other. Cunnin' as a
fox, he put his long leg in the furrow an' the short un' on the
brew. He run like a hare. Never did kitch 'im!'

Over a pint of ale in The Red Lion, Ken and I were
discussing the sorry silence from the Metropolis; for Big Ben
had gone on strike by refusing to strike. I suggested that, as
Ken the Cop stood six foot four inches in his cop-socks he
should proceed smartly to Westminster and wind up Big Ben,
for he could almost reach it without his thatching ladder.
Little did I realize that within nine months I would become a
clock-winder.

The tragedy struck, unlike our church clock, for Roy Frewin
our clock-winding specialist got himself translated to Saffron
Walden, leaving our fox-hunting parson Eric Wheeler to wind
the clock when ill and smarmed with the sores of shingles. In
the public bar of The Red Lion, where affairs of international
consequence are discussed and settled without undue action,
landlord Alec Basham chipped in during dominoes. First he
looked at his watch, then at the clock in the bar. Both were
telling lies. He addressed the multitude. . . .

'Do you realize that we've been without time for nigh on a
month. The Vicar can't wind the clock, he's too poorly. How
about a couple of volunteers?'

There was a double-tap on a table. Not from a volunteer,
but from a disappointed domino-player. He had no 'fives' and
the deck was 'fives about'.

'I'll give you a dig, Alec. Come on, we'll do it now,' said I.

'Can't leave the bar, Vera's out. Anyway I ain't got the key to the tower. Tell you what, we'll do it tomorrow. Be here about nine!'

Alec the landlord and little me opened up the door, climbed the tortuous stair and put a delicate pair of hands apiece on the handle of the massive winding-wheel, and began turning. All we had to do was to adjust the hands to make up for nearly a month's lost time. After about forty turns of the great heavy wheel the weights rose about two millimetres. We sweated, I swore, and Alec said, 'There's no need to go on so. Patience, patience!'

We were at it a long time. Bells rang for every change of hour. Puzzled villagers peered and pondered, wondering if they'd missed a wedding, funeral or christening. Was it the Alarm, the All Clear, an Invasion or just a Saint's Day?

Our hands were blistered, our shirts soaked with sweat but, before we descended from the tower completely, we stepped through a tiny window to the roof, to see if the hands were telling the truth, and they were: the whole truth, the most welcome truth. It was 10.30 precisely – 'opening time'.

When we learned that Roy Frewin had gone for good, we appointed a new clock-winder. Guess who? . . . You've got it! PC Ken Marks volunteered to mark time for us. He started last week and managed to squeeze his bulk up the crooked stairs like a Camps End ferret after a Shudy Camps coney, From all accounts he wound the clock wheel like ordinary mortals wind wrist-watches, 'twixt forefinger and thumb. He put a foot wrong though. Somebody asked him why the church clock was slow.

'Blast it! I didn't look to check,' said Kenneth. 'My watch is broken!'

If you want to know the time, don't ask *our* policeman!

20

My Market Guru

O, Suffolk is a noble county, full of lovely views, miss
And full of gallant gentlemen, for you to pick and choose, miss;
But search the town all round about, there's nothing can compare, miss
In measurement of merriment with Edmundsbury Fair, miss.
    Then sing to Bury, merry town, and Bury's merry mayor too;
    I know no place in all the world old Bury to compare to.

                                                (A Bury Fairing, 1851)

To arrive in Bury St Edmunds at any time, in any season of
the year, makes the heart rejoice, particularly the heart of a
Suffolker. Other folk hold it in the highest regard: poets,
writers, musicians. William Cobbett who did much rural riding
thereabout summed it up in eleven words: 'I take Bury to be
the most attractive town in Suffolk.' James William Addison
said much the same in different words, but he, too, used eleven
words: 'To alight in Bury is to feel that you have arrived.' You
would never believe it, but when I spoke to PC Ken Marks
about Bury St Edmunds, I also used eleven words: 'It's about
time you took me to The Nutshell at Bury!'
    Out of police uniform and in a hurry Kenneth arrived at
our bungalow next morning. He wriggled his rump into
one of our new armchairs and hollered, 'Coffee break!' Vera
shot into the kitchen and soon shot back, coffee and cake-
laden.
    'Are you off duty, Ken?'
    'Yes. Spike told me he's not been to Bury market for over
fifty years. Because he's as nutty as a NAAFI fruit-cake I'm
taking him to Bury and I'll clap him in The Nutshell.'
    'What's The Nutshell?'
    'The smallest pub in Britain!'
    'Bring me some ham and tomatoes. Don't have too much!
The last time he was in Bury he shouldn't have been there at

all. He went to Haverhill to get me a loaf of bread and didn't come back for four days – and without the bread!'

'You'll get your ham and tomatoes; I'll take care of that!'

Ten minutes later we were Bury bound. Scudding, dizzy clouds like wisps of lambs' wool seemed to beckon us over the border. Nature had painted a patriotic picture along verges and hedgerows with the scarlet of poppies, the white, tall, waving cow parsley and that heavenly blue flower of linseed. Over the bridge we saw the sign of Suffolk, at Wixoe, the source of the Stour. We dawdled through Stoke-by-Clare, 'Proud' Clare, Cavendish and Long Melford. Just past the Constable-pink, juice-of-the-sloe-stained cottages of Cavendish – so pleasing to old Duggie's eyes on our earlier venture – I saw the sign pointing out the road to Glemsford. I gave an involuntary gulp: unsure whether to feel ashamed or guilty, for passing the place of my birth. Presently we were in Bury: more quickly than we found space in the market car park. What joy it was to jostle in the market precinct where motors were not permitted! To jostle and gossip with sons and daughters of the soil; to hear the rich dialect while trying not too deeply to inhale the rich, ripe smells. As a former professional spreader of dung I could determine the differences. Top of the Pongs was the essence of pigs, closely seconded by a blend of ferret and rabbit, goat and stoat. Kenneth and I leaned on five-barred ash-wood hurdles to watch pig shepherds prodding prime porkers into pens – to a chorus of grunts and honks, screams and squeals.

I spotted the merriest pig-prodder: a hulk of manhood whose big body seemed too small a casket to contain his obvious enjoyment of life. He wore blue jeans, wellies, and a T-shirt used for advertising Abbot ale, a strong bitter beer brewed at Bury by Greene King. In bold letters the T-shirt proclaimed – I'VE JUST SWALLOWED AN ABBOT. Having been a soldier for twenty years I am reasonably swift at spotting other ex-soldiers, and I liked the cut of this prodder's jib. I prodded him, near his belly button, and said. . . . 'That T-shirt is telling lies, metty. By the look of your gut you must have swallowed the whole monastery. Were you in the Guards?'

He looked at my tie. He put out his hand to shake mine. His eyes measured me from top to toe.

'You're not far out of the ground,' said he, condemning my full height of five foot nine inches in highish heels. 'You're not big enough to have been a Mick!'

'I was not in the Micks, I was in the Royals, now amalgamated with the Blues. I rode horses, not armoured cars. We did not develop our bodies at the expense of our brains!'

'Ride horses? Your lot! If they locked you in a railway carriage you'd fall off before you left the station!'

He told me that he had served in the Irish Guards and had been wounded when the German Panzers broke through at Sedan – when the Guards Armoured Brigade suffered heavy casualties. I told him that I had been a 'donkey walloper', the Footguards' nickname for the Household Cavalry; that unlike his foot-slogging fraternity I had never proceeded to places on foot.

'I was in the Band, I knew your Director of Music, Colonel Jiggs Jaeger who commanded me to write a book about the Royal Military School of Music, Kneller Hall. I wrote the book and called it *The Band Rats*. It was published after Jiggs died and I dedicated it to his widow. . . .'

'Well I'm buggered. You must be Spike Mays!'

We shook hands. I took his address. Later I sent him a copy of the book.

Wearing the bracelet of a Guru, a lily-white turban and a saintly beard, there stood at a nearby stall a sari-selling Sikh: an old man with sorrowful, kindly eyes. He seemed quite startled when I addressed him in Hindi and gave him the Sikh valedictory greeting; but he returned the greeting, we swapped hugs. Kenneth and some lady onlookers were consternated. The Sikh was so pleased, and so was I, for I had served with Sikhs during a five-year spell of service in India; for a time in the Punjab (The Land of the Five Rivers) before India was separated by the creation of Pakistan. I quoted bits of the *Shabad*, a Sikh hymn, 'Miya pyare noon' (Dearest Lord).

> Go now and tell our Dearest Lord
> The state of His yearning disciples.
> Without Him our soft beds are hard, like stone.
> Our water-pots, our water-pots
> Have become like sharpened spikes.

The rim of our drinking cup
Is like a dagger's edge.

'What's all that about?' said Ken. 'If we don't hurry we'll
be too late for one at The Nutshell!'

Bury is renowned as being the storehouse of the whole
history of the county of Suffolk. Even from prehistory there are
magnificent displays. Picks and mace-heads from surrounding
districts abound, together with crude farm and domestic implements. There are Roman relics – coins, brooches, spoons
– and finds from the Anglo-Saxon cemetery at West Stow:
brooches, necklaces of glass, bowls, vases and urns. Near the
entrance of Moyse's Hall there are other relics: the Bury labels
and billheads – fine examples of typography. They include
relics of William Corder, the Polstead murderer. He took over
eight minutes to die. His death was watched outside Bury Gaol
before an audience of many thousands. After his execution by
hanging, his body was placed on a trestle table in Shire Hall,
for public exhibition.

Rightly reputed to be the smallest pub in Britain, The
Nutshell is also crammed with sightseers and other relics –
hatpins, helmets, guns; packets of Victorian cigars, snuff-
boxes, pretty pictures of faded ladies, and a five-shilling packet
of halfpennies. It was more crowded when Kenneth squeezed
us into that tiny bar, not much bigger than the village lock-up
at Steeple Bumpstead.

'Two pints of Abbot!' ordered Kenneth, and in less than
two minutes we were served. The day was hot, the beer tepid
and expensive. Kenneth didn't quite kneel to quaff his pint,
for as a policeman he was used to crowds. Only a contortionist
could drink with ease, so we did not have the 'other half', but
left – on ham and tomato safari. I halted when I heard a yelling
. . . 'Honi soit qui mal y pense!' The French noises came from
the mouth of a tall shoe-seller who had spotted my blazer badge
and wished to brag about his regimental motto instead of doing
his civilian duty – selling very good leather shoes at half the
price charged in pukka shoe shops. He was a Suffolker, the
shoes, Yugoslav; he had been a Warrant Officer in the Coldstream Guards.

'Were you in the Coalies?'

PC Ken surveying the scene

'No! Donkey-wallopers. Before your number was dry: March, 1924!'

'Want a good pair of brogues, senior soldier?'

I did, but he had not my size. (A year later he was still there. Now I have a pair of first-class brown brogues. I have christened them '*Honi soit*'.) Kenneth was growing somewhat restive. . . .

'We've had Irish Guards, Bengal Lancers, Coldstream Guards. If we go back to the market there's a stall where you can get fire-guards and trigger-guards. After that you've only to meet the Home Guard, then you'll have met the bloody lot!'

I bought tomatoes from a stall. The fruit and vegetable stalls were sights for sore eyes, all at their ripened best, and flowers were everywhere. I thought of my father who had served many years in the county regiment and had been stationed at the old Gibraltar Barracks, now the headquarters of the new amalgam of the Royal Anglian Regiment. He loved the beauty of Bury and its flowers.

'Do you know, boy,' he began, when he was very ill. 'When I was stationed in India, at Landi Kotal, I sometimes thought of Bury St Edmunds, and I fancied I could smell the roses and honeysuckle. Once you smell them in Bury, you never forget it!'

'It's just down here, near the crossing,' said Kenneth. 'Greta always gets her ham here, it's home-cure, the best ham in Suffolk!' And well it might have been, but his wife Greta will never get it there again. The shop was boarded up.

'Bugger me!' said Kenneth. 'Come on, we'll get some at the cold meat counter at Woollies.'

We selected ham and queued to pay a lovely lady operating the one-note electronic cash till, behind two equally lovely ladies who were jabbering away in Welsh. I addressed them in Welsh and asked them to sing '*Calon Lan*' . . . I pitched the note and off we went. One verse, then a few bars of '*Cwm Rhondda*'. There's lovely! Other customers clapped, including the electronic cashier whose machine produced a bill.

'I shall not pay unless you give me a kiss,' I said.

She did. I paid up. Kenneth hustled me out.

'What the hell are you two doing in Bury . . . you're out of bounds. Get back to Steeple Bumpstead!'

'As soon as we've had a bite to eat I'm taking him back,

and I'll clap him in the lock-up. What a day I've had!'

The gentleman so concerned about our infiltration was also
an ex-soldier. Gordon had a farm at Ashen, near Stoke-by-
Clare. During the Second World War he served with my
youngest brother in both sieges of Tobruk and along the
Chindwin with Orde Wingate's Chindits – they were in The
Pompadours (the Essex Regiment).

'Let him out for the Meet, Ken. Thurlow and Puckeridge
are meeting at The Red Lion, Steeple Bumpstead. . . . See
you then, take care!'

From a flower-festooned fish shop we bought chunks of
white-flaked cod, fresh from Lowestoft, with sizzling, golden
chips chopped from King 'Teddy' potatoes. There were tables
and chairs and dimply smiles from waitresses with bloom on
their cheeks and smoulders in their soft eyes. My escort would
not let me sit down to eat . . . Hellabit! He thought I might
speak to someone. Instead, I had to do a 'take-away'. He drove
me from beautiful Bury towards Steeple Bumpstead, until he
found a haven, a seclusion. We ate our fish and chips, using
fingers, not forks: piping hot from grease-proof paper.
Double-wrapped in pages from *The East Anglian Daily Times*.
All alone. In a lay-by!

'What do you reckon to Bury?'

'Kenneth, old pal, I loved every minute. Thanks for taking
me. I will never forget the people we met today in that good
old Suffolk market town!'

'Nor shan't I . . . all bloody foreigners! Stuff that greasy
paper in the glove compartment. We're off!'

There's nothing else in jollity and hospitable fare, sir,
That can with Edmund's Bury and its famous Fair
　　compare, sir;
and guests are very welcome hospitality to share, sir.
　　For beer is brewed and beef is bought
　　For Edmund's Bury Fair, sir.

Then sing of Merrie England, and roast beef –
old English fare, sir. . . .
　　A bumper to the Town and Trade
　　of Bury and its Mayor, sir!

21

Probing

'The very chap I wanted to see. Lovely mornin' ain't it? Now then, what are a-goon ter hev alonger me, Teddy, met?'

I intended to tell the gentleman that he had the advantage of me, but he kept on nattering about fetlocks.

'She's bin a-standin' in har stall most o' the week. Har hocks are all right, I reckon, but she's swelled up ag'in on har off-fore. Tell me, Teddy, what'll I do?'

Never before had I been addressed as 'Teddy'. Ever helpful, I did my ex-cavalry best. . . . 'Try a cold compress on the pastern, between the fetlock and hoof. Make sure the frog and hoof are clean; it could be an infection, possibly "Thrush"!'

'Thankee, Teddy. Landlord, top him up!'

The saloon bar door of The Bell Inn, Haverhill, opened. Through the door came Teddy Burgen, Haverhill's veterinary surgeon. I had never seen him. He had never seen me. When I looked at Teddy I seemed to be looking at myself. Identical twins could never have done a better look-alike.

'You must be Spike Mays,' said Ted the Vet. 'I've heard about you from your brother Les. We are alike, aren't we?' I agreed, and told him that now I'd seen him I hoped to grow out of it. 'This gentleman seems to be needing your help,' I continued, pointing to old Fetlocks.

Fetlock was fair flummaxed. . . . 'Bugger me! Could hev swore he were you, Teddy, met. Do you know, the pair on ye are the spittin' image o' that owd Captain Mannering in *Dad's Army* . . . Miraculous, bloody miraculous!'

I never saw Teddy Burgen again. Shortly after our brief meeting he died. Brother Les helped to carry him. I was told by Ted Sissons, my pork cheese expert. . . . 'D'ye know Spike, owd Teddy 'ont die while you're alive, met. We shall hevter call *you* Teddy now!' Quite a number of the old 'uns do. Makes me sad and pleased at the same time! Mostly 'pleased'. I have met Vets!

There sat I with Albert Andrews, with whom I attended school at Helions Bumpstead before World War One. We were speaking of old times in The Three Horse Shoes, of when Helions had five pubs, and when men were men, and women glad of it; when fields were full of horses, men and women, and not a tractor in sight. Across the bar a hatch opened to disclose smartly-dressed, gladsome gents who appeared to have celebrated. The younger yelled at me. . . . 'Where did you get that tie?'

'My wife bought it for me.'

'Do you know that it is the tie of the University of Edinburgh?'

'Yes, I do!'

'Did you go to the university, if so, what did you read?'

'Yes, I went there and I read a lot of books. Any more questions?'

'Good! We'll come round.'

They picked up their glasses. They joined us in the spit and sawdust bar. Mr Harrison introduced himself and his colleague, Mr Manctelow, Haverhill's Veterinary experts. 'We were at the Royal Dick Vet at Edinburgh. Did you know it?'

'I knew it well. I read English and Industrial Psychology and I shared digs at No. 1 Leamington Terrace with a Vet student named Joe Fraser, who is now the senior veterinary officer of Edinburgh. He would have ploughed his exams if I had not helped him in his study of tadpoles and beetles!'

'You knew Joe Fraser!' There's bewildered they were! But I had shared digs with a mixtie-maxtie of Scottish and English students: five sixth-year Medics and a brace of Vets who were learning useful things about ants and elephants. Between them they kept me in moderately good health – the Vets playing the major role. When they felt like getting their heads down for serious study – usually when they were out of funds and had not the 'latch-lifter' to enter The Golf Tavern for the wee-ist of wee drams, they subjected me to abuse: calling me Professor Skinheid because at forty-five I was Edinburgh's oldest student, but a bit short of thatch. I had to ask them questions from their perishing text-books, then tell them the right answers, from answers at the back of the books, if they stood a snowball's chance in hell of graduating. These occasional sessions of study were dubbed 'poverty probes'. From lurid pictures in their surgical treatises I learned of other probes: mind-boggling, nerve-shattering, blunt and sharp-ended instruments for boring holes in defenceless animals. I liked the picture of that long stiletto for digging deep, and thought it might come in handy for extracting the price of a wee dram from the hairy depths of Joe Fraser's sporran.

I discovered another probe merchant in Steeple Bumpstead. His name was Joe, but he was not a Fraser, but a Findlay. Rum owd lot, these J.F.'s! Findlay's penchant for probing became internationally recognized. One evening when Vera had popped out (while *Crossroads* was still on) I switched to another channel: just in time to catch the tail end of a pro-gramme called *Probe*. A familiar face lit up the screen, a Steeple Bumpstead face. It was owned by Sir Peter Kirk, who for many years lived in our village, attended our church and represented us in the House of Commons as the Conservative member for Saffron Walden.

Sir Peter was being grilled, questioned and probed about the EEC, the Common Market, for which he had worked so long and well, by a covey of cunning and highly intelligent scholars. The programme was extremely interesting. Sir Peter answered every question, frankly, honestly, without resorting to 'party politics'. I was so impressed that next mid-day in The Red Lion (our pub where the main topics of intellectual debate are sex, religion, politics and goggle-box) I praised the *Probe* programme and lauded the scholars. Joe Findlay was present. Ex-Group Captain of the Brylcreem Boys, who smirked as I spoke.

'I'm so glad you liked the programme, Spike. You have met those sixth-formers when you gave a talk about East Anglia at Saffron Walden High School last year. They are my lot. I was there with them, and we have just got back!'

I had been twice to his school. Once to talk, and once when I was invited to attend by Major Brian Keeling, Director of Music of the Blues and Royals: the Band in which I had played which was touring East Anglian schools. It was he who introduced me to the pupils and staff as an old member of the

band. It was I who introduced Joe Findlay to the whole of the
band – 'Joe Findlay, Gentlemen. My bowling partner. The
worst bowler in Steeple Bumpstead!'

Joe was no mean prober. Blessed with humour, joviality and
the keenest of intellects, when not playing dominoes, cribbage,
or bowling with me, he probed his large garden with fork, hoe
and excavator. When fruit and vegetables had matured he
would mount his rusting bike to deliver the products of his
horticulture, free of charge, to the old and ill. Doves flew over
his old cottage, ring-tail, fan-tail. I made him a dove-cote
with midget roofs over each entry. To me, a masterpiece of
carpentry! Joan, his good-bowling wife, brought it back. She
was apologetic in manner; such a kindly, smileful rejection!
'They keep out the rain, but they also help that old tom-cat
get in!'

The Red Lion's tap-room was known as 'The Discussion',
wherein could be seen seated parson and poacher, gamekeeper
and grocer, millionaire farmer and pensioned-off peasant.
When conversation lagged, Joe sometimes introduced some
form of history: a subject he was suspected of teaching at
Saffron Walden. I let myself into a torrential diatribe when I
told him there was no future in history, that he would be
gainfully employed by taking a correspondence course in
snooker, tennis or darts. Following his snort of disapproval, Joe
proceeded to put me in my ignorant, non-historical place. . . .

'History is nothing to do with the "past"! History is happening. There are all kinds of happenings – all the time. Where
there is no happening, there is no history. Got it? Let me
simplify for thick-headed cavalrymen. . . . To become history
all the happenings, or events if you like, must be related
together to form a chain, a continuous flow. You should know
that. You have written for newspapers. You have written
rubbishy books!'

'Thank you, Joe. You have my permission to return all the
signed copies you scrounged. If you bought one, that would
be history, or perhaps a miraculous precedent!'

'Belt up! To write even the simplest story three factors
are indispensable: the connection of events; relatedness to
something or other, or someone; and an understanding of mind
which appreciates the coherence and creates the concept which

means a meaning. There is *no* history without meaning or chronological sequence!'

'Thank you, Joe! Chronologically speaking you're next for drinks. It's ancient history when you bought the last. But first, I will shoot you down in flames about chronology. . . . When my first book was published, the publisher gave me a lot of words on the chronological caper. "Mr Mays," he said. . . . "You are a natural writer, but you have a contemptuous disregard for chronological sequence. You have not said where and when you were born. It should be said on the first page or, at least, in your first chapter."

'I borrowed paper and pen and wrote what seemed to be required in my best handwriting and suggested it should become the opening sentence. . . . "On August the 5th 1907, I was born at the age of nothing in a bungalow at Glemsford, Suffolk. My mother was present on that occasion. She is now dead and cannot testify."

'You will see, Joe, that I did not exist until I resorted to chronological sequence; even though I was standing smack in front of this important publisher and had been knocking about this wicked old world for sixty-two years.'

'You are dense. . . . You have missed the point, but I do understand. If you had been given three brains like the one you are trying to use, you would not qualify as a half-wit. Get my pint!'

Steeple Bumpstead Bowling Club has two playing teams, 'A' and 'B'. Our HQ is the tap-room of The Red Lion: a pleasant, friendly joint bristling with inter-service and inter-regimental rivalry. Most of our male members are ex-servicemen: some are sons of men whose names are deeply chiselled in the grey granite of our war memorial. We are fortunate in sharing the wonderful community spirit of the bowling fraternity with that inexplicable comradeship between men who have shared common dangers. The same spirit is evident in the bowling clubs of other East Anglian villages and is immeasurably and magnificently manifest at the end of each match. Each player buys a drink for his opposite number: quite often more than twice. Each member commands his wife, mother, girl-friend to provide haversack rations, and not to forget cheese and onion sandwiches (by far the favourite) and sausage rolls. Toasts are drunk, prizes awarded, raffles raffled and songs sung. I have yet to find a bowls club where, in the sing-song, there is not included in the musical menu vocal renderings of 'Tipperary' and 'Lilli Marlene'. Much work is needed, and gladly given: Jack Bacon, Bertie Willett, brothers Eddie and Brian of the tribe of Haylock, keep the green in snooker-table order. Ian pushes the pen as club secretary, and Joe, God rest him! used to draw up the fixture details. . . .

Almost three years to the day when he introduced me to the perils of chronological sequence, and one day after we had played together in the 'B' team, we sat for our Sunday pint. Those, like me, who attend church first, call this Sunday quaffing 'The thirst after righteousness'. I had been to church. Not Joe, he'd been knocking out our 'B' team fixture list.

'Good morning to you, King Farouk!' said Joe on my entry. . . . 'You will be delighted to learn that we are playing against our Egyptian tribe next week. We're off to Glemsford. I'll pick you up at six o'clock sharp. Your woods are in my car.'

King Farouk was only a lad when I was in Egypt and the whole of the Egyptian Navy was named after him. A gun-boat called the Prince Farouk. His papa was on Egypt's golden throne during that time I was in Cairo, from 1927 to 1929: old King Fouad I. He cut up rough over Palestine's creation and refused to accept or recognize the credentials of Lord Lloyd. He changed his mind when my old regiment, the Royal Dragoons, ringed his palace with drawn swords at the slope, five live rounds in our Lee Enfields' magazines and one 'up the spout'; and the Gunners of 'L' (Nery) Battery of the Royal Horse Artillery had aimed their biggest and best on the lowest central portion of his jewel-encrusted drawing-room.

I informed Joe, who was not delighted about my Egyptian bulletin. So, I enlarged in chronological sequence. . . . 'Just after old Condy's Fluid (the cavalry soubriquet for Fouad I) saw sense I was sent to Heliopolis, where your Brylcreem gang had two squadrons. The bomber squadron flew Handley Page bi-planes; the fighter squadron flew Bristols. We (cavalry regimental signallers) taught them how to snatch messages from the burning sands. How about that, Joseph, m'lad?'

We had a drink apiece. Joe looked to his watch. 'It's pudden time. Joan has made us a steak and kidney!'

'Snap!' said I. 'Vera has made one for me. Come on, let's not be late.'

We walked Church Fields together. We both had our steak and kidney pud. One hour later my telephone rang. It was Joan, distressed and incoherent. Joe's historical probing had been nipped in the bud with a heart attack. I felt much alone at Suffolk's Egypt!

'Little Egypt! All cod's-wallop and old mawthers' tales! Glemsford was called that through mythology. . . . All lies!' Eddie Blake, our Jack-of-all-trades and village Walter Mitty would believe nothing in which he had not taken part: like being hurled off Wembley's 'wall of death' three times without a scratch.

I told him that mythology, like his vivid imagination, had its own truths and was reckoned to be the study of religious or heroic legends so strange to the limited experience of ex-Lambeth layabouts that they could not possibly believe or understand what was obvious to clodhoppers. Until London children were evacuated to dodge Zeppelins and Gotha bombers in the First World War they believed that milk was brewed in Nestlé's tins. They had never seen a cow; and when I took my Tottenham cousin to Langley Wood one evening the noise of a screech owl scared him into filling his pants. He thought it was a ghost. Glemsford was by no means mythological: it had long been a stronghold of Liberalism, whereas Long Melford was reputed to be fanatically Tory-minded. Ninety years ago party political weekend wars broke out. Saturday night-fighters of Glemsford used to 'cut across the fields in hobnailed boots to Melford, to have a political punch-up with the Mat Makers. On the next Saturday the Mat Makers would cut across the fields in the opposite direction to return the compliment.' According to my late friend Ernest Ambrose's book *Melford Memories*, 'After the battles, the gutters ran with blood. . . . Most Suffolkers know Glemsford's nickname. Few, if any, know why it was so named; but the names Glemsford and Egypt have become synonymous.'

Fifty years have passed, much water has passed under Kasr-el Nil (The Gate of the Nile) since I left Cairo in 1929. But here am I in Steeple Bumpstead's Lily Corner, where I had a chat with a brace of fellow Egyptians. Where once were undulating meadowland and pastures pleasant, a big dig has begun, not unlike that one at Gizah when Carter & Co. unearthed the forepaws of the Sphinx and discovered Tut-Ankh-Amon's tomb and sarcophagus half-way up Cheops, the biggest of the three shining lights of the East. I thought I was on to something big. Could I have discovered distant relations of the builders of Cheops!

One fine morning, unlike Arabs who fold up their tents and steal softly and silently up on you in the dead of night, a brace of fellow Egyptians cluttered up my skyline: Ted Oakley and his brother Ray, hard-working builders, born and bred in Glemsford. They were not alone; that is if you can count mechanical contrivances as 'company'. With them was a met-allic monstrosity: a digger, with crab-like claws, a shovel like the cow-catcher on a Yankee troop train, little claws like those on Llanelli lobsters and a scorpion-like tail of scarlet steel. Before our villagers could say Cleopatra they straightened up our lovely crooked stream that trickled over Church Street. They then dug deep into the bowels of Bumpstead, after swiping the fertile top-soil. Into these deep cavities they poured from another machine as long as Edgware Road incalculable gallons of porridgy cement.

'We're makin' a concrete base for the bridge,' they said.

'*Bridge!* . . . We don't want a bridge!'

'You're gettin' one!' they said. They were right. We needed it for the water that cascaded from the footings of the new estate-to-be, and the water that overflowed through the straightened-up little river – so that we could keep on having floods. We never had them when our nice little rivulet was crooked and we were bridgeless.

Being Suffolkers they meant us not a happorth of mischief. They had Council orders – from Essex! They were kind to me. I only 'suggested' that a mite of rich top-soil would ginger up my godetia plants. My fellow Egyptians had earlier brought more mechanical monsters into play. With dumpers and bum-pers, hoists and cranes they had piled up into pyramids top-soil, bottom-soil, hoggin, gravel and ballast. Next morning at eight o'clock when it should have been light, it was dark. My fellow Egyptians had taken the hint. In front of my window was a pile of top-soil, a midget Cheops. Vera was delighted. We shovelled away most of the day. Vera with a teaspoon-like fire-shovel. Talk about sweat! I had to see Dr Fleming.

'I have a nasty pain.'

'Where?' I pointed. He stuck his finger into peculiar places. He asked me to cough, and I did.

'Hernia! Do not lift anything without bending the knees,' he said. I decided to lift a pint of bitter without bending my knees. Otherwise I had not the strength to carry a verbal message. I went home. Despite the non-lifting command I picked up my saxophone and played a few bars of one of our regimental marches – the Egyptian one, *Aida*. Later in the day I told the Oakley brethren of my indisposition. Ted expressed concern and regret and gave me an invitation.

'I'm just off to Glemsford. Hop in! I'd like you to meet my father.'

It turned into a memorable morning. His father and I got on like housen a-fire, and they all promised to bring me off-cuts of plywood, to help in my toy-making for our village children. I did not like to ask Oakley senior if he had taken a hand in building Cheops. He looked younger than me.

Little Egypt called me back home by television recently. I just had to see again one of Suffolk's colourful personalities. My friend Richard Seabrook has been a shepherd since boyhood. He now owns 1,100 sheep, grazing in Ickworth near Bury. He is President of the East Anglian Sheepdog Society. He has a lovely wife, five children and three border collies, Moss, Kep and Tess. They live in Glemsford Vale, whence can be seen towering the prominent landmark, Hartest Church, for which Richard helps to toll the bells. He is a master bell-ringer. One daughter plays the church organ, another sings. It is the church to which I was invited to preach the sermon for one Harvest Thanksgiving. Richard was one of the speakers at that Horkey Supper. I was another. He is in constant demand as an after-dinner speaker for he has a rich dialect, a wonderful sense of humour – plus a limitless fund of Suffolk anecdotes – and he sings . . . 'If you ain't heard owd Richard sing "Farmer's Boy", you hain't heard nawthin'!'

I hitch-hiked from Steeple Bumpstead to see him. I just had to – after watching the profoundly moving television series he was in, with shots of our county like Constable landscapes.

Richard was out with sheep and dogs when I arrived tired and late, but delighted. I did not hitch-hike back. After cancelling a speaking appointment Richard drove me home. He gave me an autographed bottle of White Horse . . . 'Do you look arter they owd ship!' My hitch-hike was, like the television series, a labour of love. Like the theme music . . . *Parlez moi d'amour* – whully beautiful!

22

A Battery of Baptists

If Granny Ford were alive today, she'd fetch me a tidy clout of the ear. Granny was not a 'Devil-dodger': she was an out-and-out dedicated Anglican, was church-christened at Bartlow church, Cambridgeshire, and would not attend any other except for Harvest Festival. She had been christened, confirmed, married, and would be buried at Bartlow, as would her husband and several of her twelve children. For fifty years she had walked two miles back and forth to Bartlow church each Friday to clean, dust, scrub and polish it: for love, not money!

Grandfather Reuben might also land me a clout of the ear if he were still around. He worn't much of a churchman. Being a horse-keeper he hadn't got the time, but he was no 'Devil-dodger'. Once a fortnight he would walk to Bartlow church and back for equally selfless reasons – tools over bent shoulders – to tidy verges, rake grass and paths and tart up the untidy, neglected graves. He never went to chapel!

I went to church with my father and brother Leslie: twice each Sunday, plus once more for Sunday school. I still have my old *Hymns Ancient and Modern* to prove it, with strange verses written in it by fellow choirboys long since dead. . . .

> Matthew, Mark, Luke and John,
> Bless the bed that I lay on.
> Four corners to my bed,
> Where four angels nightly spread.
> One to watch and one to pray,
> And two to carry my soul away.

There is an entry about William Tuck, our Ashdon school-master:

Old Willy Tuck, that be his name,
He goes to church on Sunday;
And prays to God to give him strength,
To cane we boys on Monday.

But we went to Ashdon church in those days when it was well-filled, with far more men than women at the morning service. Sunday's dinner was not only a meal but a challenge. Women would be hard at it while the rest of the family were worshipping.

There was social discrimination in the church seating. The squire had a pew at the front. Farmers, according to acres and affluence, sat behind the squire. Ex-soldiers of commissioned rank, Captains Reville, Lucas and Collins, would be about two horses' lengths behind, on the near-side, facing the altar. Such professionals as postmaster, grocer, baker and other tradesmen would be on the off-side, their social standing indicated clearly by the degree of proximity to the wooden, spread-eagled lectern. Last the children. . . .

'Child'en should be seen and not heard!' That was the doctrine of some villagers, but in Ashdon church, children could be seen – and heard – always seated farthest from the pulpit, many of them ill-clad and under-nourished, in the last four rows of pews nearest the vestry. Leslie and I could see the lot from our superior seats in the choir-stalls.

Now and again wicked choirboys used to beetle off to Ashdon's Baptist chapel. They would try to gate-crash their tea parties, which we called 'bun-struggles'. Sometimes we would sneak into the highly religious magic-lantern shows, just to watch for mistakes. The man in charge used to thump the floor with a billiard cue to announce the next picture: '*Jerusalem!*' he would holler, but ten-to-one it would be Nazareth or Bethlehem.

If our parents got to know, as they invariably did, we were in for a good hiding. Churchmen should *never* go to chapel, they said . . . 'It's Devil-dodging!'

Lots of us used to 'Devil-dodge' and nip smartly to the baptisms at Ashdon Baptist chapel up Radwinter Road. Under the floorboards of the rostrum lurked a large tank of water reserved for Baptism – by total immersion. The process was

Father and mother, with Les, Spike and Poppy

irreverently described as 'that owd sheep-dippin'' by which villagers had been initiated or made members, sometimes at the ripe age of seventy years, and young girls in white night-dresses were held under water 'not arf long enough' as Gordon said. He had four sisters!

When I was a boy, the Rev. T. H. Smith was the Baptist minister; he had been at Ashdon since 1896 and stayed until 1920. He lived at the manse, up a narrow and stony lane. His livelihood was precarious because he was entirely dependent on his flock. Although they came in droves to his chapel, like Pastor Smith they were not over-blessed with riches.

The Baptists were always tolerant and welcomed visitors to their church and social gatherings. Return visits to All Saints', on the other hand, were regarded by the Church of England congregation as deplorable antics of Nonconformist Devil-dodgers.

Although I was christened at Hartest, re-christened at Helions Bumpstead, confirmed at Saffron Walden, and part-ordained in Steeple Bumpstead's village pub, The Red Lion – to preach for the pub's Harvest Festival – I've always had a soft spot for the Baptists. They seem to be more human. Maybe it's because they don't hit the headlines or wear a lot of coloured nightgowns and sashes.

I was mighty pleased to meet a whole shower of them one March a few years ago at Ashdon Baptist Church, and to hear that the Baptists have at last got a rise in wages, without going on strike or picketing Anglicans, Presbyterians, Roman Catholics, Brahmins and Buddhists. At least five parsons were on parade, some with their dog-collars at the high port, but all wearing welcome and happiness on their faces. This was the Reunion because one of the Baptist tribe had delved into archives to discover that way back in December 1809 the Reverend Matthew Walker and eleven members of his congregation formed themselves into a church and fitted up a place of worship – on the site of the present Sunday school – the very place where we used to gate-crash the Baptist bun-struggles. As usual, they catered for the inner man. Tables groaned with the weight of good home-made food, and winsome women whisked round the hall with cups of tea and direct orders that one should meet everyone else. The walls had faded sepia photographs of the village and villagers, albums of photographs and ancient news cuttings.

'Fancy meeting you after all these years.' . . . 'Remember when we got caned for scrumping?' . . . 'I've got twelve grandchildren.' . . . 'People didn't hev much in them days, but we were happier by far. You could leave your doors open, no need to lock up, met. Dussen leave 'em unlocked today!' . . . 'Know what I miss most? The hosses, and the men an' women on the fields. Life ain't a mucher on the fields now. No company, but yew don't git wet on a plastic-covered tractor!'

The former parsons gave us a wee chat. All paid tribute to the village of Ashdon, and its villagers, and invited us to their Reunion weekend services on the following day. The Reverend Harry Chapman, who is now retired and living in Norfolk, was the first to address us. Speaking of the changes he had noticed on his return, he picked on one of his former Sunday School pupils, my good friend Kenneth Marks. . . .

'What a surprise!' said the Reverend Harry . . . 'Look at him, he's now a good six foot five, and I have a job to look at him away up there. I used to bend down to him and lay my hands on his little shoulder.'

'And round my little ear'ole!' quoth Kenneth, and the little Sunday School room rocked with laughter. We had the modern 'magic lantern'. We had an excellent slide show of photographs old and new, and of the villagers old and new. There were no catechisms, no collects, no lessons or creeds, and nary a sermon, but the goodness of the Baptists took one by the heart. And on that night we dodged the Devil – he didn't stand a chance!

23

Rest on Your Arms Reversed!

One October day both tap-room and saloon bar of The Red Lion were buzzing with comments about yet another financial crisis . . . 'There's allus bin a crisis with my money,' said Joe (The Tap). 'Never did hev half enough on it. They financial experts of the BBC hev bin yappin about it fer days. Dunno why they git all wukked up. You see they young varmits, politicians an' all, yappin twenty ter the dozen about poverty. All wearin' suits costin' more'n a hund'ed quid, they can't be farin' too bad, but they ain't never done nothin'. Not one on 'em could do a day's wuk in the fields. They couldn't knock a wire nail in a bit o' soft wood without hitten' their bloody soft fingers!'

'Yew ain't far off the mark there, Joe. Let's hev another pint afore the buggers put it up ag'in. Can't git two pints fer a quid now. We ain't half a-comin' to suffen!'

The essential characteristic of money was discussed (eruditely) in the saloon. By farmers reluctant to open purses in case the moths escaped; by a bunch of entrepreneurs who had infiltrated Haverhill from London, to become deputy managers of new firms in the old Industrial Estate. Their thesis was that money is set apart from all other known substances. It was not desired solely for itself. Nobody, it was said, perhaps with the pathological exception of the miser, desires to acquire oodles of the stuff: except for the purpose of some day paying it away again in return for goods and services of exceptional value. Cecil was extremely interested. Before his recent translation from nearby Castle Camps he had flogged expensive furs – in Mayfair.

Some were profoundly concerned about the rise in the bank rate. One who had not enough of the ready to buy a drink (known as The Joiner) postulated that he had completely lost his former interest in money. . . . 'After my bankers discovered that I was endeavouring to exist on the interest of a hitherto undisclosed overdraft, their interest in me as a person declined. Their misery increased when I informed them that human beings had the capacity for happiness long before money was invented. They refused to enrich me, or fill my glass which as you now see, Gentlemen, is empty!'

Although the entrance to the churchyard is but ten short paces from the front door of The Lion, and one can check the shout of 'Time, Gentlemen, please' by the church clock merely by peering through the window, no mention was made that a bob or two would come in handy to the Spiritualists – from the monied Spirituous. One needed to be garbed in oilskins and southwesters to sit through a short sermon and remain dry. Our church roof was giving up the ghost.

The year before the Rev. Eric Wheeler had squatted on a seat outside the church, facing The Lion, from nine until five, collecting the root of all evil from passers by, and made about £450. But now he was laid low with shingles.

Unlike Chancellors of the Exchequer and others of that ilk, our villagers took turns to collect the money. It was not unlike 'guard duty'. I did my stint with Colonel Deakin – two hours on and four off. We scrounged a lot of money. Not one farmer with short arms and long pockets was allowed to escape our attention.

Later, I reported to the Vicar. We did not waste words speaking about money, nor about the political party jamborees at Blackpool and Brighton. We spoke about horses and the Horse of the Year Show. I suggested that he was not suffering from shingles, it was a girth gall – because he had tightened his belt far too long. His reward for saving souls was less than folk get paid for being unemployed, but Eric wished not to talk about it. So we switched to the ailments of our four-legged friends. . . . thrush, strangles and glanders.

'Glanders is incurable,' said Eric.

'I know,' said I. 'I will tell you a story about it.'

I told him about Anthony Gilliat, one of our charming young officers of the Royal Dragoons, who tragically was killed by a tiger on a shoot in India. Some years before, Gilliat had been a Troop Officer under the Command of my Squadron Leader, the late Colonel Wintle.

Gilliat had been warned about Wintle. Fellow officers told him that Wintle was somewhat unorthodox: that he occasionally dressed in dinner-jacket, overalls (cavalry, not mechanic's!) and swan-necked spurs, and went off on long bicycle rides deep into the jungles of the richest Maharajahs. . . . Soon after Gilliat arrived from the UK, the regiment were sent some remounts from the famous Remount Depot, Saugur. Our vets disliked them so much that they were returned to Saugur, where it was found that they had developed 'glanders', a terrible disease that is contagious and can be transmitted to human beings. There was then no cure for it, either in horses or men. The whole of our regiment was put into isolation. All horses in the squadrons to which these horses had temporarily belonged were ordered to be malleined. This is an injection into the neck of a horse: not a prevention, but a test. If the horse has been infected, the injection provokes a characteristic swelling which indicates that the horse has incubated glanders and has to be destroyed.

One day at breakfast somebody said to Gilliat, 'As those horses sent back to the remount depot were in your troop, you will have to be malleined as well.'

Two days later Gilliat asked, 'When do you think I shall have to be malleined?'

This, of course, was right up the street of cavalry officers, far too good to be true! Fellow officers told him incredible stories about this malleining lark. Some said it was done in the arm, others in the leg, but as sure as God made little apples the limb would drop off in six months. Gilliat was sent to the Veterinary Hospital, Trimulgherry, to be malleined, to a vet who had been forewarned, and who told him he could not jab him straight away as he had only enough stuff to do the horses, but was expecting an early consignment from Bangalore. All agreed that it was scandalous that horses should be considered before officers. He was also told that vets used the same needles for men after jabbing them in horses: that the whole business was insanitary.

Soon everybody in the garrison heard about it and helped with suggestions, but the joke became tiresome. The officers then invented a special Veterinary Officer, one Major Wetham-Botham (pronounced 'Woofram') who had arrived overnight from Poona to mallein Gilliat. He had won the Victoria Cross in the Great War for malleining horses under shell-fire. He had been shot in the mouth. His voice was seriously affected. He hated speaking to people and disliked them speaking to him.

Then a captain, Alfred Daniel Wintle, was promoted to be the mythical Major Woofram. He had taken on a bet for a tenner that he would persuade Gilliat to part company with his trousers, and would prove it. A note in Gilliat's locker read: 'Please report at 1100 hours to the outhouse at the end of HQ Squadron lines for mallein injection B2. Trousers must be worn, not breeches. (Signed) J. G. Wetham-Botham, Major, RAVC.' The recommendation was so that he could change from breeches into trousers, which he could whip off without a boot-jack. Gilliat was warned not to upset the testy major.

'Don't ask questions. Just do as he says!'

Gilliat changed into trousers and arrived at the outhouse. A bed had been put in the room. A bowl of potassium permanganate and some bandages were on a table alongside a huge bottle half full of a deadly-looking liquid labelled 'Tinct. Malleini B2'. A powerful smell of disinfectant pervaded the outhouse, and there stood Major Woofram, in a white smock, wearing rubber gloves. A white cap covered his hair, a white mask covered his mouth and nose, and a pair of dark spectacles his eyes. He was beaver-busy manipulating an enormous syringe which would have been capable of quenching a major conflagration. The Major nodded briskly. In a peculiar voice which was caused not so much by German bullets as by a couple of pebbles he had in his mouth, he asked Gilliat to sign a form on which the word 'horse' had been crossed out and the word 'officer' substituted. Through pebbles and mask he barked at Gilliat. 'Sit on that bed. Take off your trousers!'

Still absentmindedly holding his syringe, Major Woofram picked up the trousers, shuffled along to a door behind the red screen, then raced like a scalded cat to the Officers' Mess. Complete with trousers, syringe and a signed certificate he was in time to pick up his tenner and produce to a bevy of subalterns about to mooch off to 'morning stables', Mr Gilliat's pants.

'Spike, it's either too good to be true or too true to be good!'
He was cheered. His eyes shone as he leaned painfully to pat
my shoulder. 'You are keeping me alive. Hand me my drink!'

'It's not me, Master Skypilot, 'tis the whisky and milk.
You're taking too much milk with it. Cut the cow juice, double
doses of John Barleycorn and you'll live for ever!'

'I do not wish to live for ever and I shall not. From the
moment of birth we begin to die. Some take longer than others
I've noticed, and I've certainly christened and buried a few.
Do you know, Spike, I've been doing just that for the last
twenty-five years, in Steeple and Helions. Years ago the
labourers could not afford to marry: they lived together in sin.
The villages were nicknamed Sodom and Gomorrah. The
villagers had many children which, as the legend goes, they
used to share out each Christmas with the raffle. Incest was
rife and it was difficult to determine lineage; whom and what
belonged to tother and which. Parsons used bribery to raise a
congregation. They promised to marry the engaged and
'spoken for', free, gratis and for nowt, if they would attend
church twice every month. People were so poor that parsons
used to give them a copper or two to put in the collection. It
is also said that Sunday school children used to pinch a coin
or two, even in church; hence the verse:

> We goo to church on Sunday
> To hear the parson shout.
> We slip a farthing in the bag
> And hook a tanner out.'

I informed the Rev. Eric Wheeler that I was aware of the
facts (and fiction). That I had lived in both villages: first in
Helions, before he started his primitive errand on Yorkshire
moors. That I was born in Suffolk and had not descended from
a long line of unchristened bachelors.

'Come on, Toby!' Eric nodded gratefully, as I took his dog
for a walk.

It was not only the villagers of his own parish who had a
profound regard for Eric as a forthright, practical Christian.
He had critics from Newmarket and Thurlow, the homes of
East Anglian horsemen and foxhunters; some of whom de-

clared that beneath his medal-ribboned surplice he sometimes wore his hunting gear, with jodhpur breeks and riding boots – even when in his Steeple Bumpstead pulpit.

When he arrived in Essex his two village churches were in disrepair, almost dilapidated. He made no appeal. He rolled up his sleeves and often single-handed sawed stout roofing beams, retiled the roofs of both churches, repaired and faced up defaced masonry and rebuilt church porches and pews.

As he had forecast before the Hunt Saboteurs' violation, his church filled up. He continued to write his parish magazine, staple it together, pack it in road delivery stacks, and deliver it door-to-door on Shanks's Pony. Ironically, after all the to-do about hunting Eric could no longer ride. Crippling arthritis put a stop to his gallopings and he was fast declining.

One fine evening he drove me to see Suffolk's fine churches – Lavenham, Long Melford, Cavendish and Clare. Afterwards we decided to have a 'stirrup cup' in The Bell Hotel; to have a word with its proprietor, Hugh Jones from Llanelli, also a good horseman.

'Spike, my friend, we are living on borrowed time,' said Eric. 'We have served our allotted span of three score years and ten. Before this year is out we might both be out.'

'Cheer up, have a drop of port!' (He liked it!)

'Now then,' said I . . . 'Tell me where we shall end up if we both go out before the year goes out. You should know, you're the sky pilot!'

He pointed to the ceiling.

'We shall be up there, where all good horsemen go!'

'Will we be happy?'

'Not at first. We shall be sitting on our silver clouds, playing our golden harps. Our nightgowns will be whiter than white, our wings perfectly preened, and we shall be wearing our haloes at the regulation angle. We shall not be missed. Five minutes after the heavenly quartermaster has kitted us out we shall look down to earth from the edge of our silver cloud.'

'Where? To Steeple Bumpstead Church?'

'No! To The Red Lion.'

'Not before opening time, I hope.'

'Oh no! Our old friends will be there, playing dominoes. Bert Willett, Bill Willett, Ted Haylock and Joe Findlay. Then

Jack Bacon the roadman will go in and enlighten them. . . .

   '"Hev yow heard the news, tergither?"

   '"What news?"

   '"The Vicar an' Spike both died this mornin'."'

Eric tried to look solemn, but failed. He continued. . . .

'Their reaction would be typical of all domino-players. . . .
"Pints all round. Whose down is it?"'

Three weeks later I walked past Claremont, the house owned
by ex-cattle king, Les Humphries, standing opposite the vicarage. Les sometimes looked over his wall to watch Eric's golden
labrador keeping a sharp eye on him from the wall opposite.
Toby was not on wall-watch, but Les came up to me. He
looked very upset. Like most countrymen's his words were
brief, yet spoke volumes.

'Eric's gone, Spike. He'll live for ever in Bumpstead!'

I was deeply upset. The words of Dylan Thomas thundered
in my mind . . . 'And death shall have no dominion'.

Later in The Red Lion, after the news had got round and
Mrs Wheeler had said there were to be no flowers, landlord
Alec Basham said: 'What, no flowers! Well, if that's what Eric
wanted, that's fair enough; but I'll tell you this. . . . If they
hadn't been told, the villagers of Steeple and Helions would
have packed Church Fields with 'em.' And again my mind
flashed to the words of Dylan . . .

> Where blew a flower may a flower no more
> Lift its head to the blows of the rain;
> Though they be mad and as dead as nails,
> Heads of the characters hammer through daisies;
> Break in the sun till the sun breaks down,
> And death shall have no dominion.

Our village was numbed. We had lost a central and colourful
character, a practical Christian, when Eric died on that July
afternoon. We learned he had offered his body to the medics
for research, thinking it might do some future sufferer a good
turn. Money would be wasted on flowers he had said, 'Give it
to the Church'.

There were flowers, jungles of colour and perfume, messages
of love and farewell – mostly from women, who brought

armloads and carloads from villages and townships local and remote. His memorial service was attended by nigh on a thousand. Bishops, Deacons and top brass parsons flocked like sheep and were folded in the choir stalls. Some came just to bury our Caesar, not to praise; but Eric's good was not buried with his bones.

Phil Barnes, nigh on ninety, a regular church-goer and Old Contemptible of the Great War, was not impressed by the mitre-wearing fraternity. . . .

'Pity they didn't come when he was doing all the work on his own and his missus worn't up to much.'

We sang for him, to his favourite chant, his favourite Psalm 121: 'I will lift up mine eyes to the hills. . . .'

On the wall of Bendyshe Hall, our village home for the old ones, there is a plaque. On its near-side verandah, a sturdy memorial seat – alongside Church Fields, where our children play and buttercups grow. Les Humphries worn't far off the mark. . . . 'He'll live for ever in Bumpstead!'

24

Decline and . . . Fiddlesticks!

Renowned city-dwelling social anthropologists and other desk-bound pundits have wept and muttered untruths into their tangled beards. They reckon that the decline of the village is one of the tragedies of English history. After a couple of pink gins, instead of good Suffolk ale, they get more depressed and mumble that this decline is no less tragic because it is largely unrecognized.

We do not recognize it in Steeple Bumpstead for a very simple reason: the decline hasn't started! But the pundits continue, in lecture halls and clubs, in posh hotels and city pubs, to prophesy and postulate that our prospects of revival or survival are dimmer than a modern Toch-H lamp. . . . 'What is the social order of the countryside?' they demand. . . . 'What does the future hold for England's villagers?'

Now then! In this part of East Anglia, where most areas are sparsely populated and the bulk of our rural population live in villages, the answer to the pessimists' questions can readily be found. It is among the older villagers that real 'social order' exists. They and their forebears have set the standard. This is the basic meaning and purpose of the village community, for it provides not so much the facilities and amenities of our lives but, more important, that corporate sense developed from close proximity, daily association and understanding. Everyone knows who's doing what and when and, if they do know not why, they will soon find out.

In the country nature determines our living patterns, health, jobs, personal habits and recreations. In the townsmen's lives the pattern is artificial. He has no need to defy the weather, the townsman. His routine is regularly planned, his leisure and entertainments are mostly manufactured, and he is less dependent upon the goodwill of any neighbour he might happen to know. Thus, because of many organizational advantages, he has more time on his hands to develop his alleged superior intellect. . . . But what of the poor, dim-witted 'declining' countryman? Despite increases in his material comforts he puts far less trust than the townsman in the inventive cunning of man. He has profound respect for the natural and elemental forces on which the cycle of birth, life and death depends, and this is the key to his self-reliance and individuality.

Long before the oil barons of Arabia bought up Belgravia, the communal life of the village was characterized by its close connection to the soil. Our forebears practised fertility rites, danced to and even worshipped the elements: hence the origins of the Christian Christmas and mumming plays, and the folk dances that once composed the dramatic repertoire of the village. We had real songs then, songs about the loves and labours and sorrows of country life, like the annual joys of Harvest Home. There were songs about sport, poaching, drinking, wenching, dancing and death – and carols. Singers toured the villages and fairs on foot; especially the Hiring, Mop, or Statute Fairs, named after the Statutes of Labourers issued in the fourteenth century which (like today) sought to pin down workers' wages by regulation. Yes, we had real singers and real songs.

Like other East Anglian villages, Steeple Bumpstead's non-existent decline is on the up-and-up. We intend to survive as a living community, not as a collection of fossilized stones. We provide food for the nation on our fertile fields and a large proportion of our own amusements which, insofar as they are home-produced, do not interfere or compete with the attractions of nearby towns. We carry enough oil in our rustic lamps to enjoy both.

Take for example the Bumpstead Fair which took place one May. At the last minute, without consulting a committee or the Prime Minister, they switched the title to Steeple Bumpstead Carnival Fayre and listed items on the posters so numerous and varied that lack of space precludes any attempt by me to classify or define them.

Nevertheless, a couple of hitherto unknown events took my eye and were perpetrated by a strange tribe named 'The

Danglers and Dumplin's', a motley bunch of East Anglian lads
and lasses who had studiously researched some peculiarities of
our past and produced them for village entertainment. They
hailed from all walks of life, but were united in their pursuit
of the traditional. Over the years they had attended many fairs
in East Anglia, where they have sung, danced, tumbled and
acrobatted like cascading Cossacks. To keep up to date and
conform to the current norms of sexual athleticism they have
nurtured a new Suffolk hero, 'The Suffolk Stud', a very strong
young man who has developed his body and prowess to such
a standard that he proclaims with conviction . . . 'I ain't had
no complaints so far!'

We were confronted by covens of witches; terrified by tortu-
rings, maimings, stool-duckings and killings. Comely village
maidens were enjoined to assist 'Mad Mick' break his own
world record for 'Jumping the Maidens'. Our young men had
to prove their manhood in the arenas of 'Welly Flinging' and
'Dwile Flunking'. The whole of the assembly strove to witness
ancient trials by the notorious Judge Jeffreys who was on
parade with a battalion of vicious criminals. There was not
room for all in our ancient Moot Hall where felons appeared
before His Lordship for trial. All were condemned to death
and justice was meted out to them later. Their necks were
stretched (in mime) on the Bumpstead gallows, in public, with
one near miss: a slip-knot refused to slip and poor Gregory
was nearly garrotted.

The village hall worked overtime: a grand dance for all, a
tea party for children aged two to seven years and a disco for
teenagers. Just to let Ipswich Town Football Club know they
worn't the only lot who can kick a bladder of wind into a
pig-net, the gentlemen footballers of Thames Television flung
out a challenge to our Steeple Bumpstead FC.

Thames Television brought along Outside Broadcast vans,
took pretty pictures of our pretty village, entered every event,
provided most of the prizes – and won the beer-drinking
competition. Their infiltration into the peace and tranquillity
of our lives was due to two of their gang sufficiently cunning
to own houses in our village: John Parsons, who owns a row
of cottages opposite my bungalow, and the late Tony Simpson
who had a lovely cottage just behind those owned by John.

We will all miss Tony Simpson, especially on Sunday mornings. If not busy making films in London he would be in our church, singing well and clearly after ringing the bells. Tony never graduated in the science of campanology. Not that he needed to for our church, for the bell-cords are plucked in a box – none of this plush rope-climbing stuff. I doubt if Tony ever heard of 'change-ringing', a system of complications invented in England at the beginning of the seventeenth century which involves a patterned changing of the order in which the bells are rung. The dab hands at this delightful art have dubbed it 'musical mathematics'.

Although he was never guilty of patterned changing, he undoubtedly introduced changes never rung before in an English church. We could tell when he was back in the village. There are not enough bells to do justice to each note he wished to ring, but one could determine from the first six notes of 'God save our gracious Queen' that comedian Tony Simpson was patriotic. One was reminded of Justice, perhaps Usury, by the next five of 'When will you pay me, said the bells of Old Bailey'. Between these two he sometimes interposed obtainable major notes of well-loved hymns – 'Now thank we all our God, with hearts and hands and voices', 'Just as I am, without one plea', and 'The day Thou gavest, Lord is ended'. The next phrase coincided with the opening notes of Llanelli's famous rugby song, said to be the third national anthem of the Land of the Leek . . . 'Sospan Fach'. It was so strange to hear on a Sunday morning in the peace of Steeple Bumpstead's Church Fields as the swifts and swallows darted over the new-mown hay in landless flight. During his penultimate release from the tribulations of television we met in our post-office. Tony's eyes sparkled, his straggly white beard wobbled as he clasped my hand.

'Ah! my dear friend, Spike. Good morning. Please take this!' He handed me a £10 note. 'Kindly give it to Major Corry. Tell him it will help to pay for Eric's memorial seat.'

Tony was on parade at Church Fields when the memorial seat and plaque were 'unveiled' and the brand-new sports pavilion built by our hard-working and clever Argent lads was officially opened. Usually gregarious and talkative, he was reticent and strangely quiet. He looked so ill and frail that shoulders were found for his support. He could not ring the bells. He could not sing.

Tearfully, Jacky, John Parsons' wife, came to my bungalow.

'Oh, Spike! Tony has gone. Such a lovely man. Our wonderful friend! It doesn't make sense. John sends his love, he's too upset to come over!'

Good people keep popping off, but the village lives on. Even before the Carnival Fayre had ended, plans were afoot and schemes were hatched for the next year's rejoicing. The Braintree Carnival Committee and the Essex Young Farmers had drawn plans and sites for numerous side-shows. Wellies would be slung, dwiles would be flunked, musical recitals given and Church Fields would blossom with hydrogen-filled balloons. There would be Morris dancing, maypole dancing, bun-struggles, every kind of sport, and the Braintree Marching Band would be counter-marching and drumming away as if on Horse Guards for the Queen's Birthday.

But the carnival is but an annual outward and visible sign of the inward and spiritual grace of our village life. It goes on all the time without display. Without this innate kindness and concern the annual stalls could not be packed with works of village art, nineteenth-century paintings, exhibitions of old Rural England. Not to mention slate-engraving, horse-shoe nail-engraving, weaving, tapestry and corn-dolly-making; enamelling and jewelry; displays of dried flowers, strange stone-craft – all mucking in with rag dolls, miniature clay fruit and Steeple Bumpstead pottery.

'We shan't goo dry at the next Fair, metty,' said one village ancient. 'The postwomen towd me that Greene King are lookin' arter the gravy!'

Yes, life will still go on in this declining village! We shall have processions through *our* village of *our* villagers all dressed up in carnival costume; of vintage motor-cars driven by veteran men; and the programme will close when our senior citizens sit down to more strawberries and cream (and maybe more champagne) as they listen to the Saffron Walden Ladies' Barbershop Harmony Club.

It has occurred to me that the 'dismal Jimmies' are telling a great untruth when they say that villages of less than a thousand population are unable to afford the upkeep of all the services,

Trainee shepherd with Suffolks and dad

amenities and those institutions that give a village a strength and character of its own. There is not enough work, they say; not enough custom for village trade, not enough patronage of village societies, not enough children for the primary schools, not enough life. They sum up by saying that these are solid facts that cannot be abolished by mawkish sentiment, or by making appeals to the ancient heritage of village history.

If the Social Survey of Steeple Bumpstead undertaken in 1978 is to be believed, we are a mite below the thousand – by one hundred and fifty bodies. We seem to have afforded the upkeep of the essential services and institutions. We certainly have a strength and character of our own. Very few are unemployed, so there must be work going on somewhere. The village societies lack not patronage – just try to book up the village halls! And as for 'not enough children for the primary schools' . . . Well, I never did! We have three schools chock full of very lovely children.

We have a new vicarage, with a new parson in it, the Reverend Mansfield. His wife is not quite unemployed as schoolteacher, Sunday school teacher and general factotum for church goings-on. They have started a children's choir. They teach the gospel with chalkings on a blackboard and by example.

We have new landlords and ladies in our two pubs, who do not complain unduly about lack of patronage, for they cater for bowling clubs, cricket clubs, football clubs and darts and dominoes clubs. The Royal British Legion holds its meetings in those pubs as do Barbershop Songsters. Our new shop 'The Shopping Basket' or Steeple Bumpstead general stores, gives magnificent service and prevents senior citizens ambling a couple of miles to Haverhill's super stores to purchase inferior goods at superior prices. Our chariots for 'meals on wheels' have passed their MOTs and continue to deliver fodder to those unable to cook, stand or walk. Our Women's Institute is busy constructing Jerusalem in Bumpstead's green and pleasant land – and making enough jam each year to fill the fête stalls, free, gratis and for nowt. Members of our 'Over 60 Club' keep busy amusing each other and appear to look younger each time we clap eyes on them. Our young married gals are too busily engaged in the process of reproduction to form a

Mothers' Union; thus we have more prams than pamphlets, and will possibly have to build another school.

Since the day I retired and returned to Anglia to rest I have been kept so busy that I have wondered how the devil I managed to find time to go to work. Days are not long enough to cram in a mite of leisure, and retirement is a very busy business.

For sharpening shears, knives, scissors on my grindstone-equipped lathe, I receive buckshee haircuts, trips to nearby towns, bottles of jams, wines and preserves and horse manure for my roses. In my greenhouse I put on my hat of seed and plant propagation, sometimes succeeding in producing healthy plants and flowers for unhealthy friends and strangers. It can be somewhat disappointing. For years I grew gorgeous godetia, luscious lobelia, monstrous marigolds, splendid salvia, adorable alyssum and perfect pansies.

Cecil Beale ('There is a green hill') stated in public that my pansies were superior to others grown elsewhere. He scrounged lots of them, gave lots to his children – who now boast about them in places remote. I became pansy-deprived and wrote off to the seed merchants a letter of complaint. In the month of February, pansy seed planting time, I filled box upon seed box with Pansy 'Swiss giant mixed'. I watched and watered duly but they did not ripen to my need.

PC Ken Marks, professionally trained in observation, was the first to spot the error. He reported to me by telephone.

'We are having salad for lunch today. I'll be along in a minute, so pull me a couple of pansies!'

My stiffish letter to the seed merchants threatened relentless litigation under the Trade Descriptions Act – for deliberate falsification; disguising vegetables as flowers; making an honest son of the soil a bloody idiot in the eyes of his village community. Pansy seeds were put in: cos lettuce came out.

Swifter than USAAF-guarded warheads could be launched at the Red Army Choir from peace-loving Lakenheath, or any of the many other Suffolk townships which now have a tidy crop of nuclear carrots, there came from Boston (Lincs.) more seeds. Both lettuce and pansy, with apologies galore and instructions profuse and without charge.

I was cheered. Life seemed to be brightening. For nine

weeks Vera had got herself 'shingle-struck', as they do say, and remained in agony and a flimsy nightie because she couldn't even bear the light touch of East Anglian air.

'Where hev she got it, Mr Spike?' asked Mary, a fellow shopper.

'Started in the middle of her back, and it's now galloping round to her front.'

'Oh, dear me! Tha's bad. They do say, yew know, if that meets in the middle, both ends a-joinin' up, yew'll die.'

On return from the village store I commanded that Vera should lift her nightie. She seemed mildly pleased, but quite surprised! I ran my builder's tape round her shingle girth and enjoined her to make the most of what she yet could spend. According to Bumpstead folklore she had only an inch and a quarter to live.

New seeds are ready for their February planting. Vera is present, but the shingles have gone. Bursting with energy after nine weeks of idleness, it occurred to Vera that a tidy coat of white emulsion would tidy up that bit of kitchen ceiling that went brown after I burned a saucepan or two. She sloshed the stuff on. I told her to stop; that the wooden step-ladder was not safe (I knew because I made it), but up she went and like a poor horseman dismounted without permission. Small bones became dislocated in her off-hind and she broke the ankle for good measure. She wore plaster of Paris puttees for twelve weeks and plodded around on crutches.

With influenza, residual bronchitis, high blood pressure and shopping baskets, I beetled off to the village store. Friend Mary was on parade. . . .

'How is Vera a-gittin' on, Mister Spike?'

'Fair to middling, Mary. A great improvement, she's only got foot and mouth disease now.'

'You're pullin' my leg!'

'You know she's got a bad foot, but you know what women are: the minute they begin to get better they start nagging.'

'I shall tell her what you say!'

'Don't you bother, Mary. I told her before I left for shopping!'

'Well, I never did!'

Yes, the year took its toll. Our Senior Citizens and British

Legionnaires have been dropping off like flies. Maybe it's because they turn up in cold churches and stand at cold gravesides to say their goodbyes to old friends; then catch a chill and become next in the queue for a coffin. One recent departure saddened me. The former landlord of The Globe public house at Clare, Jack Stiff, died, following an accident in a motor-car. For years he was secretary of the Clare Horticultural Society, after serving his pontoon (twenty-one years) in the army and becoming a sergeant major. Gardening was his delight, together with fishing and shooting. He was chairman of the Clare Charitable Trustees and a part-time fireman, and did a mite of good to anyone he thought was in need of it. The Globe was a kind of sanctuary for ex-servicemen. Women were not welcomed, and Jack ran the pub as though he was conforming still to military law!

'Thirteen hundred hours, lads! It's pudden time!'

And Jack would not serve a gill until he had eaten the food so wonderfully cooked by his wife. Nor could a trace of Jack be found in the pub on Sunday nights until *Songs of Praise* had been televised. He considered it to be a wonderful programme for sorting out the wheat from the chaff, and because he loved the old hymns.

Jack died twice. When the news of his former demise leaked out, customers, friends and strangers had a whip-round to buy his funeral flowers. Some say it was a news reporter who had put a foot wrong and had mixed up names. Anyway, when Jack emerged from hospital and was able to sit near his telephone, he had a kind of roll-call. From florists and other espionage agents he wheeled out the names of those who had ordered the flowers and invited the lot to a never-to-be-forgotten Resurrection Party.

Jack's departure reminded me of grandfather Reuben Ford's words to me when Auntie Harriett died and I was seven . . .

'People come, and people go. You lose a friend, you get another, boy!'

Grandfather worn't far off the mark. When the Reverend Eric Wheeler died I lost a good friend, but found a replacement soon afterwards when a 'foreigner' infiltrated Steeple Bumpstead. He had been looking for me for some time, he

said, because I had written about Suffolk, he said, and he
wrote books as well, he said.

We fair took to each other and, as sure as God made little
apples, I began to tell him about Suffolk, bearing in mind
grandfather's bit about people coming and going. I informed
my newly found friend that all sorts of people had been coming
to and going from this part of England long before he barged
in. That long before Romans arrived on our Saxon soil (and
hung around until we turfed them out in AD 436), we had been
pestered and suffered intrusions from unmentionable tribes:
the French, Rhenish and Belgic squatters. Gangs of Angles
then pushed in, all the way from Holstein, and started political
party games of division. They split themselves into North
Folk (Norfolk) and South Folk (Suffolk). One hundred and
thirty-nine years later (AD 575) East Englia (whither I have
returned) became the Kingdom of East Anglia, and what a
kingdom! A land of trees, flowers and skies. And what skies?
Never the same for two hours on the trot: they infatuated,
obsessed and intoxicated Constable and drove lesser painters
round the bend.

'Oh, the skies!' said my new friend. 'That's the main reason
for me coming to live in Suffolk. Not now, but when I've
finished my time.'

And I was reminded of an anonymous piece I had read in
The East Anglian Magazine about Suffolk. It was called 'The
Spell of the Land':

There is nowhere quite like it in all England. It is a domain
of marshland and meadow, of windmills and watermills,
and red-roofed farms under spreading branches. Of towns,
venerable yet benignant, where the springs of centuries have
seen the swallows returning to ancestral thatches and where
the present seems no more than a passing masquerade under
indulgent and oak-furrowed gables. A region of small me-
andering rivers and ancient bridges, of strong chestnutty
horses and portly sheep, of tree-guarded villages and of
gracious churches, like lovely ships a-sail on the landscape.
A country where poppies hold carnival in June and the corn
weaves golden shawls for the fields against the shortening
summer. And on the uplands, there is heathland, with gorse

alight between the bracken and vagabond companies of pines, camping like gypsy bands among the domesticate trees. Here are the wide skies and great high-sailing clouds which Constable loved; here is that tang in the air that tells you, as plainly as the gulls on the plough-land, that over the hill are the downs, the lonely marshes, the lapping creeks and the sea.

My new friend is Fred Soper. He knows a lot about skies, and so he should because he's always messing about in them! A top sergeant in the USAAF (which in British cavalry terminology means 'A Yankee Quarterbloke with Wings') Fred writes poetry, as well as books for children, and functions as PRO and photographer for all the USAAF, as well as a wonderful gang of folk who go to endless effort to enhance already good Anglo/American fellowship. I like to think that Fred and I have contributed with our many tours of some stately homes and divers American air bases, despite Texan Fred putting a foot wrong in the village of Finchingfield.

'There'll be one hell of a crowd at Finchingfield House, I guess, so we'll go early. Our Base Commander is coming, and all the top brass from Wethersfield, Alconbury, Mildenhall, Lakenheath, and some of your RAF from Coltishall. It sure is a grand house. Owned by a guy named Watson!'

We arrived at ten for ten-thirty. Nary a car or a crowd in sight. Fred pushed the bell and the French-polished door was opened, by that guy named Watson: one who had gone down to the sea in ships and once commanded the Royal Yacht *Britannia*.

'We came a bit early,' said Fred.

'Very early! One week to be precise. We are having our party *next* Monday. Don't be late!' said Vice-Admiral Sir Philip Watson.

I got to know most of the American aircraft, all shackled down and ready to safeguard us from God knows what. We took pictures and I scribbled down a motto or two from the heraldic devices of wings and squadrons. The motto of the 10th Tactical Reconnaissance Wing is 'Ceaseless watch' and is depicted in the wing's emblem by a mock-up of the Greek god Argus who, according to myth, had a hundred eyes, half of which were always awake while the other half slept. Of all the frightening array of death-dealing aircraft I liked most the newest addition to RAF Alconbury's aircraft fleet. Designed for high-altitude surveillance/reconnaissance: sleek, bible-black and sinister-looking, it can cruise at more than 430 mph above 70,000 feet and has a range of more than 3,000 miles.

'I'll take the TR1, Fred,' said I at Alconbury. 'It's just what we need in East Anglia to keep a sharp lookout on farmers.'

'Farmers?'

'They are the varmints who have felled our trees, hacked our hedges, polluted our lovely skies with stubble-burning, poisoned the insect life and small mammals. We must stop them. If they know they are being watched, and might get fined a bob or two, they'd change their habits. They don't like forking out!'

Highwayman Dick Turpin was born in Hempstead. He used the inn as a getaway and hiding place. One can squint through his peephole in a beam where he kept a sharp look-out for Customs & Excise officers. Fred and I sat there, philosophizing about a Texan Half. Not some Yankee footballer, but a drink measure created by Fred the Shrewd to cheat landlords. On receiving a pint he would drink three parts straight away, then lick his chops, put on his charm and address the youngest or prettiest barmaid . . . 'Could I have another half, please?' The young ones would top up his non-brimming pot. Cunning landlord cottoned on. Texan Halves are much thinner on the ground.

'Yes, Spike, when my service ends I shall come and live here. Suffolk is a good place to come to. For you it must be a good place to come from. No, I mean to be part of!'

'I know what you mean. There are places folk like coming from, to get to hell out of: take Texas. You have invited me to fly with you to Texas, then bring you back to Suffolk to live and become civilized. Your kite might get struck by lightning or one of your own misguided missiles. Freddy boy, I don't want to leave, or die under foreign skies, but under the skies of the land of the high horizon with my clodhoppers on good Suffolk soil. Just like Cecil Howard Lay.'

'Who the hell is he?'

'An architect who built his own house in Suffolk in which

he lived and died. He wrote books, painted country pictures.
He also wrote lots of poetry, and the last verse of his wonderful
poem "To Suffolk". It expresses my wishes. Want to hear it?'
　'Sure, out with it!'
　And with it I outed. . . .

> When pool and stream were frozen hard;
> And cattle stayed within the yard;
> When elms were red, and ash-trees black,
> And sparrows robbed the farmer's stack;
> When tilth and farrow changed to stone,
> And hoodies fought around a bone;
> When hands were numb and minds depressed,
> And snow the naked trees had dressed,
> Said I, I will away from here
> In this hard season of the year.
>
> Yet here I stay and years go by,
> And *Suffolk* knows the reason why.